From .com to .profit

From .com to .profit

INVENTING BUSINESS MODELS THAT DELIVER VALUE *AND* PROFIT

Nick Earle
President, HP's E-Services.Solutions

Peter Keen
Chairman, Keen Innovations

Foreword by Ann Livermore

JOSSEY-BASS
A Wiley Company
San Francisco

Jossey-Bass books and products are available through most bookstores. To contact Jossey-Bass directly, call (888) 378-2537, fax to (800) 605-2665, or visit our website at www.josseybass.com.

Substantial discounts on bulk quantities of Jossey-Bass books are available to corporations, professional associations, and other organizations. For details and discount information, contact the special sales department at Jossey-Bass.

 Manufactured in the United States of America on Lyons Falls Turin Book. This paper is acid-free and 100 percent totally chlorine-free.

Library of Congress Cataloging-in-Publication Data

Earle, Nick, 1957-
    From .com to .profit : inventing business models that deliver
value and profit / Nick Earle, Peter Keen.—1st ed.
        p. cm.
Includes bibliographical references and index.
        ISBN 0-7879-5415-2
    1. Electronic commerce. 2. Electronic commerce—Management.
3. New business enterprises—Computer networks. 4. Internet.
I. Keen, Peter. II. Title.
        HF5548.32 .E188 2000
        658.4'0352—dc21   00-009885

FIRST EDITION
HB Printing   10 9 8 7 6 5 4 3 2 1

CONTENTS

FOREWORD

In business today, the spirit of invention is necessary in everything we do. Bullfighting provides an apt analogy. Whenever the bull is feeling frightened and threatened by the matador, he will consistently return to the same place in the ring. The Spanish word for this spot is *querencia*. This predictability makes the bull increasingly vulnerable, enabling the matador to come in for the kill. In much the same way, businesses today only add to their troubles if they return to their own *querencias*—their comfort zones; they simply can't do that if they are to succeed in today's increasingly competitive business environment. They need to invent new business models and move ahead quickly to capture the unique opportunities of today's wired—and wireless—marketplace. There's no going back.

Nick Earle and Peter Keen understand this and have had the foresight to put together a book that helps business leaders understand the economic drivers of what's been called the biggest change in human life since the Industrial Revolution—the Net Economy. The authors provide a framework for companies to reinvent the products, services, and even the experiences they offer to customers. This isn't just an intellectual exercise. It's an action that's required if companies are to truly deliver value and generate profits in the Internet Age.

The Net has spawned thousands of IPOs. It has created huge market capitalizations. It has made many companies very successful. It has caused many other business leaders to question their whole value proposition and to have many sleepless nights. But it's not enough to simply ".com" your business today—it's necessary to rethink your business model.

When the Net became a driving force behind business decisions, we were all trying to make tradeoffs—this *or* that. Now it's time to unify things. The winners are those who can bring brilliant synthesis between the old and the new, between .com and brick-and-mortar business, and between the old guard and the Young Turks.

Look back at what the industry looked like in the late 1990s. The world was divided cleanly into two camps: "the upstarts" versus "the establishment." On the upstart side, .coms were cobbling together new business models with open Internet technology—and then executing with tremendous speed. Today, these .coms are thinking about permanence. They're focusing on traditional mission-critical issues, things like high-availability systems and robust supply chains. They're replacing hodgepodge technology with systems that are sophisticated enough to run the stock exchange.

Meanwhile, in the establishment camp, brick-and-mortar companies took a little longer to get on the e-commerce bandwagon. Some of them missed it entirely, but others are now making sense out of the Net. They're thinking beyond Web sites and are starting to recognize that the Net can deliver any kind of information, anywhere, on any device. They're reinvigorating their offerings for a world of customers who are more demanding. They're learning how to synthesize—how to balance—two seemingly opposite ways of conducting business to gain new strengths.

From a cultural perspective, we're looking at a new kind of company—one that can marry the best thinking of two extremes and by doing so gain tremendous power and strength in the Net Economy.

Are you inventive in the way you do business? In the partnerships you forge? In how you sell? We're entering a world where creativity, daring, and a human-centered approach are the new currency. Is your business equipped to win in that world?

Look at how established companies are changing. Automotive firms are beginning to understand that the car—the product—is a platform for delivering services. By delivering customer relationship services such as in-car navigation, emergency roadside assistance, or telecommunications, car companies can deepen their bond with customers and also generate more revenue. Similarly, petroleum companies the world over have figured out that the gas pump is a platform for delivering services of all kinds. It's in the combination of the product and the service that revenue and profit are being made. It's not that the product is any less important; it's just much more useful with a service wrapped around it. Services drive the customer experience.

Here's another example: Corporations all over the world are now starting to think about turning all business processes into digital services. If one of your company's assets is your efficient procurement process, why not make money from that, too, by offering it as a service on the Net?

The revenue opportunities are there. The profit is there. The challenge for all of us is to think hard about how to make money from these e-services. Which e-services do you want to create? Which ecosystems of partners do you want to join? What services are going to define your value proposition to your customers going forward? And when, where, and how can you deliver those services to provide the best possible customer experience?

From .com to .profit: Inventing Business Models That Deliver Value and *Profit* helps business leaders grapple with these questions. The authors bring years of experience to this useful, levelheaded book. Nick Earle is an expert on business models for the Internet Age. He heads the E-Services.Solutions division of HP and has helped both HP and our many customers—in all fields of business around the world—create innovative new business models that allow them to capitalize on the unparalleled opportunities of the Net Economy. Peter Keen has focused on the intersection of business and technology for nearly twenty years as a consultant, researcher, teacher, and writer. The authors provide practical management advice that will help you take action to advance your business *today.*

We all know that constant change is necessary for survival in the fast-moving Net Economy. The changes we need to make in our business models are real. At times, it is tempting for all of us to go back to the circles of comfort we've enjoyed for years—our own *querencias.* We just don't have that luxury. The Internet has changed the pace of our business lives forever, and if we don't keep up we will slip further and further behind.

On the other hand, the business challenges we all face provide us with an excellent opportunity to truly shoot for the stars. That prospect fires my imagination and inspires me every day. I hope you'll feel the same way after learning the lessons in this book.

Palo Alto, California

Ann Livermore
President, Enterprise and
Commercial Business,
Hewlett-Packard Company

PREFACE

It's time—past time—to stop talking about the Internet as the future of business and to start talking about how to manage that business today so as to be effective as the future becomes the present. Ignoring the Internet is simply not an option. It's time to get down to business. It's time to discover the value path mapped out in *From .com to .profit.*

The question we tackle in this book is, *What can business do—and do now—to set priorities and competitive direction for being on the Web so as to provide value to customers and generate profits at the same time?* That is, How can you make the necessary shift from simply being open for business on the Web to staying in business for the long term—and inventing your value path from .com to .profit?

It is no simple journey, for the Internet business landscape is rugged, mostly unexplored, and much of it is in upheaval even as we try to set the maps on paper. It doesn't fall into any obvious, apparent pattern. That's what has made it so hard for managers. They get plenty of exhortation, hear again and again about a very few companies that have fast become fables for the Internet age, and see the business press spend more and more space on news about Internet business. The competitive playing field is overrun with new players—and the game is changing, it seems daily.

All this is obvious to savvy business executives; it is the answers that are not at all obvious. In *From .com to .profit* we help executives manage the transition and come up with solutions that work. Our focus is not on forecasts of what could, should, or might happen in the future. All anyone needs to know about the future is that the rate of change that developed in the late 1990s—what we term the .com era of Internet business—won't slow down anytime soon. Besides, forecasts don't help answer the question of what to *do* now. What executives do need to know is what we focus on in our book: the basic blueprint for strategy, for setting priorities, for creating real business value.

We now can see patterns and derive business lessons from the earliest phases of the Internet. Business is shifting from technology as supporting the business to technology as integral to the business. The technology base is accelerating the business shift from commerce to services. Technology innovation fuels business innovation. Business innovation fuels technology innovation. There's much more of both to come.

There will be new discontinuities and innovations that change the rules of the game. And there will be new games. Even so, the technology-independent value imperatives—the must-do requirements—of Internet business—are already clear. Common patterns have emerged in the diverse experiences of companies that are in very different markets and that have very different on-the-surface characteristics. Our goal is to bring these to the attention of business managers to help them cut through the fog (or fantasy) of Internet forecasts and hype and handle electronic business as *business*.

OUR EXPERIENCE AND OUTLOOK

For several years, the two of us have been working to gather more and more examples from experience and make sense of them, to tease out what is driving Internet business. Our examples come from case studies, company reports, press articles, surveys, research publications, and from our own work with companies. Based on our experience and research, we lay out what we know from the race to .com, what we can be sure of in the next phase, and what all this means for business managers in any type or size of organization.

When we talk about business models, capital, e-services, and mobilization, it's from our experiences as business participants—not from an abstract perspective. Nick, having lived for years in the world of technology-for-business, brings his perspective as a senior executive in Hewlett-Packard, a company that had to go through exactly the same management challenges and dilemmas as most businesses today, including what to do about the Internet. Like many large, established companies, HP came dangerously close to being left behind. Now HP is back in the forefront with Nick driving the Internet business strategy for the company, as president of HP's E-Services.Solutions.

While Nick addresses the point where the proverbial rubber meets the road, Peter operates at the helicopter level, scanning the territory. As a consultant, professor, and writer, his role in our collaboration is to provide the big picture and to relate both the technology-savvy Hewlett-Packard view and its own powerful e-services business model to the context of the typical company. Peter has wide experience in helping top executives across the world bring together business and technology, a challenge of long standing and now obviously a necessity that is very high on the management agenda for action.

Together, we answer the question of what business managers everywhere need to do to ensure that, whatever their firm did or didn't do in the beginning of the Internet story, it doesn't miss out in the next era, that of .profit.

LESSONS FROM THE PAST, INVENTIONS FOR THE FUTURE

Internet business is here to stay. It cannot be ignored—and a Web site is not enough. Copying the winners' strategies, most obviously by investing heavily in Web site design and operation, is not the answer—and is often an expense with no return. We've learned from the experiences—successes, failures, and yet-to-be-decideds—of the early stages of the Internet and e-commerce what is necessary to making the switch from simple

.com to .profit. The short answer? The business processes behind the Web site are critical to customized service and customer relationship building—and these, in turn, are the keys to the .profit phase of the Internet.

There is a marked difference between the business assumptions, practices, and priorities of early innovators in Internet business and the new leaders. The differences reflect the priority of relationships, collaboration, and community and are accentuated by the new technology and tools. In .profit, everything is personal and customized. Instead of relatively static Web sites (modeled on a storefront to which the customer comes), we are seeing more and more dynamic interactions—services instead of transactions. Instead of the storefront model, we are seeing brokers, agents, and electronic traveling sales reps roaming the Web, building dynamic offers on the fly, looking for special deals to bring to *you*.

After evaluating the forces and factors that underlie successful Internet business models, we see six value imperatives—the business must-do items that are the base for defining a firm's business model. It is not a surprise that these imperatives relate to the fundamentals of business: if the Internet didn't affect business basics, it would be just an add-on to the use of technology that has been growing for well over three decades. Instead, it has become a major disruption of any status quo in business. Value in Internet business—value for the customer and profit for the company—rests on a business model that responds to these value imperatives. They are what sort out winners from losers and leaders from laggards. Since value derives from these imperatives, the business model has to feed into them. It certainly cannot ignore them, or worse, conflict with them.

These six value imperatives form the core of our book—and can become the base for defining your company's unique business model, regardless of its specific strategy, industry, market target, or size. Your company will place a different emphasis on each particular value imperative, depending on a variety of factors, including its ambitions, history, core competencies, and target customer base. And that's as it should be; the value imperatives are templates—broad outlines—for shaping and implementing a business model for *your* firm. They constitute opportunities to take and warnings to heed. They are the foundation for answering the manager's question of, "So, what do we *do?*"

AN OVERVIEW OF THE CONTENTS
AND A PLAN FOR THE FUTURE

From .com to .profit is divided into two main parts. The three chapters of Part One, "The World of Internet Business," lay the groundwork, discussing the Internet and the direction we expect for the business models of tomorrow. In them, the reader will find a wealth of examples and evidence supporting the imperatives, what we see as the basis for success in the future.

In Part Two, "The Value Imperatives of the Internet Space," we discuss the value imperatives in depth, each in a separate chapter. We provide extensive examples, figures, and discussion of their management implications. Throughout, we point the way for building profitable business models that can be adjusted for your circumstances. The concluding section of each of the chapters on the imperatives includes reminders and action items, steps to get the process rolling, even as the Internet world blasts ahead to the future.

Then, in the final chapter of the book, we look to that future. We imagine (together with Rajiv Gupta, general manager of HP's E-Speak Operation) what the more distant future may hold and how we might best prepare for it now.

Taking the broad view—looking at the past, present, and future—we are reminded that the value imperatives are dynamic. Customer choices, competition, technology, and capital all affect them. There are many communities shaping this dynamic, new competitors and old competitors adopting new business models, new sources and uses of capital that reshape the playing field, and new technology that opens up fresh opportunities within a business model and even enables original models. We are convinced that—even amid all the changes—the value imperatives our book discusses in detail provide a sound and practical set of blueprints for inventing the right value path from .com to .profit.

Silicon Valley, California   Nick Earle
Fairfax Station, Virginia   Peter Keen

To the Market, for proving that .com is not enough:
from April 10, 2000, onward,
it's only .profit that matters

ACKNOWLEDGMENTS

This book would not exist were it not for the efforts, skill, and patience of an enormous number of people, whose lives connect with ours at work, in business, and at home. In looking into the future, we leaned heavily on the expertise and foresight of Rajiv Gupta, general manager of Hewlett-Packard's E-Speak Operation. Rajiv shone his brilliant searchlight ahead, described the scene in the distance, and helped us glimpse that future as we hurtle toward it.

We were most fortunate to have linked up with a stellar publishing team at Jossey-Bass, led by Cedric Crocker, vice president and publisher, Business. Amid nonstop changes in our businesses, offices, and lives, Cedric managed to keep our focus on the book with enthusiasm and energy. Together with freelance developmental editor Janet Hunter, he helped us map out and clarify the value path to .profit and on to the future. The entire Jossey-Bass team deserves high praise for their efforts; it is because of them that *From .com to .profit* now exists in tangible form. Thanks are due especially to Cheryl Greenway, editorial projects manager, and Jeff Wyneken, editorial production manager, whose calm guidance carried our manuscript through what, to others, might have seemed an impossible revision and production schedule. Paula Goldstein, art director, and Hilary Powers, copyeditor extraordinaire, lent polish and flair where it was much needed. Our thanks to every member of the team.

We are also grateful to Ann Livermore, president, Enterprise and Commercial Business for the Hewlett-Packard Company, who graciously agreed to contribute the Foreword to this book.

Each of us was supported by people at home and at work. We would like to acknowledge these people in turn.

A few thanks from Nick:
First of all, my thanks to Michelle Aquino, executive assistant and office magician. Without her, my level of sanity would be markedly lower. For getting me started and helping me finish the task of co-writing *From .com to .profit,* I would like to thank Mark Barounos and Atchison Frazer of Black Ink Media. My level of intelligence would plummet were it not constantly shored up with input from Allison Johnson, vice president of communications for Hewlett-Packard, and Keith Yamashita, principal with Stone Yamashita, the strategy whizzes behind e-services. Thanks to Liz Sizensky, director of executive communications, whose contributions got us all thinking and added much to the book.

Pat Pekary, manager of Hewlett-Packard Publishing, reviewed multitudinous drafts and received input from all quarters at Hewlett-Packard, thus making the book stronger and more accurate on many counts. Thanks to her and to those throughout Hewlett-Packard Company who offered advice, including: Steve Pavlovich, director of investor relations; Brad Driver, investor relations manager; Steve Brashear, director of corporate financial reporting; Eric Verdult, corporate finance; Jon Flaxman, vice president and chief financial officer, Enterprise and Commercial Business; Craig White, senior vice president and general manager, Financing and Complements Group, Enterprise and Commercial Business; and Keith Melbourne, general manager of Trading Hubs, E-Services.Solutions, Hewlett-Packard Company.

And a deep bow to Renate E. Kammersgard, marketing manager for E-Services.Solutions, who was key to the entire project. Without her, my contributions to the book would surely have never made it to print. Her research, valuable suggestions, and access to the inner workings of Hewlett-Packard, all with absolute professionalism and speed, were commendable.

My thanks and appreciation to Carly Fiorina, president and CEO of Hewlett-Packard Company, for spearheading the reinvention of HP—leading us back to our roots of invention, our DNA of radical beginnings. This spirit of invention, necessary for all of us to thrive and prosper in the new Net economy, is the genesis and promise of e-services.

And finally, enormous thanks to my wife, Debbie, and to our children, Laura and Sophie, who have the patience of saints for living with a dad who decided to write his first book on top of what were already eighteen-hour days. I love you guys.

And from Peter:
This is my twenty-something book, my sixth in three years on management in the Internet era and my third in just under a year. To write about the Internet on Internet time, you need a strong team behind you. Mine is more than just strong. Carey Colvin, Dale Garmon, and Merry Richardson are my much-appreciated research engine room, creatively keeping me up to date and locating many of the stories and figures that ground *From .com to .profit.*

Russell Hunter manages all my technology needs, from Web sites to videoconferencing studio to network, to the toughest of all jobs—helping the techno-inept, laptop-dependent traveler and writer survive the road warrior's all-too-frequent travails, tribulations, and neurotic fits. As anyone who works with me knows, my productivity and personal equilibrium rest on Jennifer Hunter, whom I cannot thank enough.

Roger Sattler, managing principal of Keen Education and a strong advocate for the Greater Washington community, is a powerhouse in the next stages of the Internet economy. He has creatively expanded my contacts and thinking and has always been my reminder that the real issue for the "new" economy is human values and the generation of good living in a better society.

I have many colleagues who have directly and indirectly contributed to the ideas, examples, and experiences out of which *From .com to .profit* has emerged. My special thanks go to Ron Williams of IBM; Sandy Boyson who heads the University of Maryland's Supply Chain Center; Mark McDonald, director of E-Process at Andersen Consulting and coauthor with me of *The Process Edge;* and Craigg Ballance of E-finity, Canada, coauthor with me of three books (and the worst punster—I hope—in the English-speaking global community). Cern Basher of Provident Bank has helped my stock portfolio profit from .profit insight and has time and again provided brilliant insights into .profit economics. He's a background presence throughout this book.

When your in-laws are your close friends, too, you are really privileged. Thank you to Merry Richardson and Peggy and Bill Richardson, my friends and family. My final acknowledgment, the most important one, is to my wife, Sherry, for just about everything, including putting up with my fifty-hour-a-week authoring neurosis. I love you, sweetheart.

And, together, our thanks to the broader community, to the .commers, entrepreneurs, and imagineers who have sparked this new realm of the Internet. Without all of you, there'd be no Internet age, no value to all the changes afoot, no profit for the future.

Silicon Valley, California   NE
Fairfax Station, Virginia   PK

ABOUT THE AUTHORS

Nick Earle is president of Hewlett-Packard's E-Services.Solutions organization, responsible for the company's Internet strategy, known as e-services. His team focuses on applying advanced technology and services to help businesses worldwide derive new value from the Internet. The group's mission includes forming strategic alliances with innovative companies that are building new business models for the Net economy.

Nick joined HP in 1982 from Citicorp Merchant Bank in London. He has held a number of marketing and management positions within HP's European operations and was named European marketing manager in 1993. He was promoted to vice president of worldwide marketing in 1998 and then appointed chief marketing officer for HP's Enterprise Computing Business in May 1999.

Nick holds a Bachelor of Science and an honorary Doctorate of Science from the University of Liverpool and is an honorary Fellow at the MBA Management School in Bradford, England.

Peter Keen has written more than twenty books on the links between information technology and business strategy, including the best-sellers *The Process Edge, Shaping the Future,* and *Every Manager's Guide to Information Technology.* From 1990 to 1996, he served as chairman of the

Advisory Committee on Information Technology to the Comptroller General of the U.S. General Accounting Office. Named by *Information Week* as one of the top ten consultants in the world, he has worked on an ongoing, long-term basis with top managers in leading companies across the world. Peter has taught at leading U.S. and European universities, including Harvard; Stanford; Sloan School of Management, MIT; the Wharton School, University of Pennsylvania; the London Business School; Stockholm University; and Delft University.

Peter received a Bachelor of Arts degree in English Literature from Oxford University, an MBA and DBA from Harvard Graduate School of Business Administration, and a Doctorate of Science from Marist College.

PART ONE

THE WORLD OF INTERNET BUSINESS

1

THE VALUE PATH FROM
.COM TO .PROFIT

.Com is about being open for business on the Web.
.Profit is about making money as a business on the Web.
And they are not at all the same thing.

How does a firm generate value to its customers and, at the same time, make a profit? To our minds, that is the one question concerning business on the Internet that is now worth writing and reading about. All the other standard questions about the Internet are either already resolved or irrelevant. The issue is how to get from .com—open for business on the Web—to .profit—staying in business for the long term. For example:

Question: Are we really in a new economy with the Internet at its core?
Answer: Yes. In fact, today we really need only three adjectives—*more, bigger,* and *faster*—to describe what's happening with business via the Web: revenues, customers, marketing expenses, security concerns, innovation, investment, price deals, and financial losses.

Question: Will the Internet change our industry?
Answer: Of course. When the Commerce Department issued its first quarterly assessment of the size of Internet sales in March 2000, it concluded

that they amounted to just 0.64 percent of total retail sales.[1] It excluded travel reservations and commissions for services such as securities trades, which would bring the figure up to around 1 percent. That 1 percent has changed the basic rules of competition in almost every industry in less than five years. What will be the impact when it's 3 percent?

Question: How large will sales on the Internet be in five years?
Answer: No one has a clue—and it's an irrelevant question.

Indeed, the standard questions are all irrelevant because of more, bigger, and faster and because of the impact of the 1 percent. All we can be sure of is that Internet business will grow and grow faster than the reaction time of most companies. That means that it doesn't matter if business-to-business commerce in 2004 is $7 trillion versus the reported $145 billion in 1999[2] or just a tenth of that. The management issue is, What do we do now to get on the value path to .profit? What do we do *now*, regardless of any forecast, so that we aren't taken by surprise any more?[3]

It has become more and more clear that most .com firms are lost in the crowd. They need much more than a Web site and catalog. A cautionary tale here is Value America, whose stock price dropped from $55 in April 1999, when it went public, to just over $4 twelve months later. The *Washington Post* commented that "Value America's unraveling is particularly prominent because it had been touted as a paragon of the New Economy . . . [and] seemed to have a unique handle on how to exploit the commercial possibilities of the Internet."[4] Despite its "mushrooming customer base," its storefront-only approach to Web business created problems of supplier relationships, customer service, inventory management, and distribution that left it increasingly adrift.

Value America is not alone. The .com era was mainly about generating revenues. (Value America shot up from $134,000 to over $45 million in just one year.) But revenue generation is often the fruit of massive marketing and massive price cuts leading to massive losses.

If we are to move past .com, we need to stop talking about the Internet as the future of business and start talking about how to manage that business today so as to be effective as the future becomes the present. The starting point—getting up on the Net, the race for .com addresses—

was the easy one. The tougher one has been to create value for customers amid a flood of other .coms. In this new style of business-with-technology and technology-for-business, *value*—not the Web site per se—is king. It points to a shift in both the technology and its use that is at least as far-reaching as the comparable 1980s transformations implicit in the very term personal computer. The PC was viewed as literally *personal,* a stand-alone device that had no telecommunications links. It's hard now to imagine a PC that doesn't have these; perhaps if we were starting over, the term we would adopt might be "community computer" or "communications computer." The PC has moved way beyond its origins and is now a set of very interactive tools—most documents, spreadsheets, PowerPoint presentations, and other "personal" uses of software are intended to be shared and communicated and the PC modem speed is at least as important to most users as its memory size.

The Web has changed at least as much as the PC in terms of its users and uses—in a far shorter time. Its early advocates praised it because it had nothing to do with business—indeed, they monitored any effort to send e-mail that tried to sell anything and launched campaigns against it. Then, as more and more companies started their own informational Web sites and start-ups like Amazon pointed to the opportunities of online retailing, just as the PC became a personal communication hub, Web sites became a business contact point. The main metaphor was that of a storefront that could handle more and more types of transaction: *cybermall* captures the thinking. The .com economy was a new set of stores.

Value generation rests on far more than this shift. As life with the Internet is evolving, personal Web pages, personal services, personal offers, personal association, personal pricing, personal anything that establishes and sustains the relationship is what value is all about. Here *personal* may mean individual, family, company, community, interest group, professional affiliates—any segmentation that creates a you-us relationship rather than just a buyer-seller one.

There are more and more successful players in the value game, players that know how to build relationships, manage logistics, mesh their channels, and transform their financial capital and cost structures. They are the brands of the online economy. Some of them will take years before they see profits from their investments in customers and infrastructures. And (as the Value America example reminds us) there's no guarantee that today's high flyer will not be tomorrow's failure. Yet the evidence is in: companies that focus their business models on the value imperatives for competing in this crowded marketspace and not just on the .com elements of it—those companies are generating profits. Value to the customer and profit to the company is their equation—and the subject of our book.

It's impossible even to guess at what percentage of large, medium, and small companies are in the race to .com, on the value path to .profit—or have arrived there and are moving forward. Our own best estimate is that among the Fortune 1000, about half are still racing to .com, but well aware they need to move very quickly. Most business executives of those companies openly admit they don't quite know how to make this shift. In the United States, there are mercifully fewer and fewer top managers who dismiss the Internet as not relevant to their company; in our experience, that's not the case in Europe, Asia, and Latin America. A variety of forces have combined to block the same degree of progress: the high cost of local phone access to the Internet, lack of the venture capital for small and high-risk start-ups, a social climate that does not encourage risk taking, and lack of real telecommunications competition in many countries. That's changing fast but there is as yet no equivalent Internet economy in terms of size, growth, and breadth. Around mid-1999, many previously sleepy regions of the world took off in all areas of Internet business; 2000 has seen the same Internet IPO (Initial Public Offering) fever as has marked the United States since the mid-1990s. In *From .com to .profit,* we focus mainly on the United States because it is here that we have a long enough body of experience and a large enough number of successful companies to be able to draw on in deriving practical lessons for managers. In addition, the innovation outside the United States is following very much the same path—though it may well be a steeper and faster path—since the new international entrepreneurs can draw on the U.S. experience.

For any firm only halfway through the race to .com—with Web sites, intranets, and some of its supply chain handled online—the technology issue is mainly one of infrastructure: of building it, renting it, operating it, or buying a position on someone else's platform. There's a lot of hard .com work to get done but that's a starting point only; the main agenda is business innovation. How *does* a firm transform itself in the business basics in order to be a player in .profit? How *does* it position itself for .everywhere, the time when the e-words and e-prefixes will all disappear, when we won't talk about electronic business or Internet retailing, for instance, just *business* and *retailing*? No one knows for certain—we don't either. But we do have a wealth of examples from companies that made very fast, very big, and very successful transformations. We present these not as Big Truths but as templates for our business readers to consider. You can find the parallels with your own company and the lessons to take from our examples. You can see how your situation is different and what that means for you in terms of getting down to business, what your challenges will be in turning value into profits. Now is the time to prepare, to embed the Internet in your logistics, relationships, channels, pricing, and processes so that your firm is well positioned for the future wave of business change.

CHANGE YOUR MIND-SET: FORGET .COM

Changing the mind-set is perhaps the single most important step for business managers to get moving along the value path. Seeing the Web site as in effect the generator of value reflects a .com mind-set; it looks back at the race to get a presence on the Net, concludes that Internet business is all about Web site design and operation, and that the priority is to get "on" the Web. .Com reflects the obvious: it was Internet technology that made Internet business possible. Companies that used it effectively gained a "first mover advantage" that either left established competitors stranded, as Amazon did to the entire bookselling industry, or created something entirely new, like eBay's invention of what might be termed the World Wide Yard Sale. Their success stimulated a race to get up on the Net. For a while it looked as if just adding the .com suffix to your business name guaranteed that venture capital firms would rush in to throw investment capital at you. This was all a variant of the old adage that if you build a better mousetrap, the world will beat a path to your door.

It didn't. It has been far harder and taken far longer to turn a Web site into a sustainable online business than early .com enthusiasts ever expected. There are indeed plenty of successes on the Web. Many of them are neither first movers nor Internet start-ups; of the dozen or so firms selling over a billion dollars of goods and services related to the Web, almost all are well-established blue chips, such as HP, IBM, and Intel, or already-successful high-growth firms, such as Cisco and Dell. So it can't be just the .com that explains their success.

There are plenty of failures on the Web, too. On the surface, many of them look similar to the successes. There's no obvious explanation, for instance, why one of the start-up Internet search engines, Yahoo, was able to turn itself into a power brand and quickly become profitable even though it doesn't charge its 100 million subscribers a penny, while its rivals, AltaVista and Excite, have had very varying fortunes. Why did major retailers like J.C. Penney and Sears bomb with their online malls despite their brand strength, while Amazon and eToys built a strong customer base in just a few years? Why did the upstarts win and the Fortune 100 players lose? Obviously customers saw value in Amazon and didn't in the retailers' offerings. Again, this can't be anything to do with the .com itself. Where is the value? What is the pattern?

THE SEARCH FOR VALUE—AND THE VALUE DRIVERS

It's easy to talk about the obvious need to create value in Internet business. But what exactly are the factors that drive value? If it's not the .com, then what is it? Business on the Web is so new—Amazon and Netscape are the useful mark of its inception, in late 1995—that only recently have we accumulated enough examples to draw on to answer those questions. Just the first few years of operations of a dozen start-ups provided no reliable conclusions; we needed information that spans more time and covers a very wide range and number of companies in order to start teasing out patterns. But when, as now, there are so many companies, old and new, with so many plans, claims, and business models, the patterns are hidden in the overwhelming noise. Competing forecasts, hype, and the prevalence of .com thinking add even more hubbub.

Consider the (highly oversimplified) view of the Internet business landscape shown in Figure 1.1. This lists just a few of the well-known companies that are Internet players. It includes start-ups large and small, (Yahoo and Garden.com); Fortune 1000 firms that have become major Internet players (UPS, Cisco, IBM); business-to-business hubs (Ariba, Chemdex, FreeMarkets); and many others. It includes some initiatives

Figure 1.1. The Internet Business Landscape

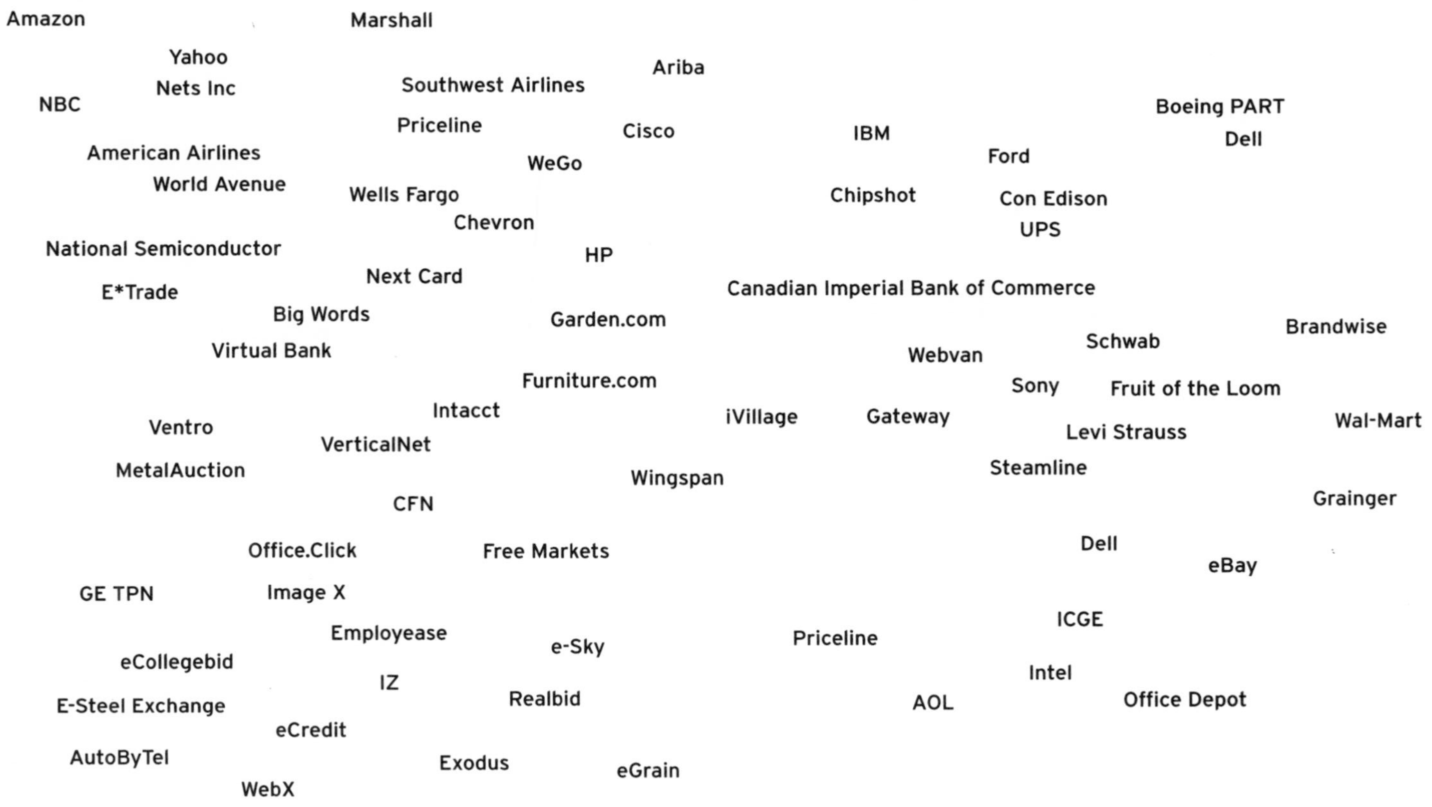

Amazon

Yahoo

Marshall

NBC Nets Inc

Southwest Airlines Ariba

Boeing PART

American Airlines Priceline Cisco

Dell

World Avenue WeGo

Wells Fargo

Chevron

HP

National Semiconductor

Next Card

IBM

Ford Con Edison Brandwise

E*Trade Big Words Chipshot UPS

Virtual Bank Garden.com

Canadian Imperial Bank of Commerce

Schwab Wal-Mart

Webvan Fruit of the Loom

Ventro VerticalNet Intacct Furniture.com iVillage Sony Levi Strauss Grainger

MetalAuction CFN Wingspan Gateway Steamline

Office.Click Free Markets Dell

GE TPN Image X Priceline ICGE

Employease e-Sky AOL Dell eBay

eCollegebid IZ Realbid Intel

E-Steel Exchange eCredit Office Depot

AutoByTel Exodus eGrain

WebX

that went broke (World Avenue, Nets Inc) and a few large firms whose first Internet strategies were less than a success (Levi Strauss); we could have added hundreds more to the picture. It includes portals, vertical hubs, reverse auctions, consolidators, ASPs, business-to-business (B-to-B) and business-to-consumer (B-to-C) firms, vortals, butterfly markets, aggregators. The very newness of the Internet business language in itself adds more obscurity to the picture.

Any commonalities among the many businesses shown in Figure 1.1, commonalities beyond the obvious fact that they're all "on" the Web, are not apparent. The figure looks not unlike jumbled Scrabble tiles waiting to be organized into meaningful words. We've been working for several years to gather more and more Internet business examples from experience and make *managerial* sense of them—to find the words hidden in the tiles. Without value, a Web site is just a money drain or technology showcase. So what is *value,* as revealed by what has actually been happening in Internet business, rather than in hype, hope, and theory?

We've found the main patterns through our search. In every single instance, value comes from focusing the technology on a number of very basic elements of business that in themselves are not at all new, but that demand a sustained and comprehensive management commitment and follow-up. They are what we see as the value drivers that should shape any firm's choice of its business model. Get the *imperatives*—the must-dos of each of these drivers—right and you create value that can be turned into profit. Ignore them or conflict with them and you're just following a .com, not a value path to .profit.

It's not transactions or price that create the value that gets customers coming back to a seller. It's relationships, collaboration, and community. Early .com retailers thought that "hits" would generate customers. They generally didn't, as IBM found with its World Avenue online mall and MCI learned from its own now-defunct initiative. Others thought customers meant profits. They didn't. Companies are paying out large fees to portals for a presence on their sites or offering large introductory gifts or discounts in an effort to attract first-time customers. But they haven't thought through how to follow up that first transaction and generate long-term relationships. .Com has largely been about transactions. With very, very few exceptions, that's a path to sustained .loss.

Here are just a few of the many implications of the difference between a business model centered on relationships and one on transactions:

- Relationship-centered business models generate very high incremental operating margins for repeat business and positive cash flows even when the firm is as yet unprofitable; in contrast, transaction-centered business models have lower infrastructure costs. Yet they must build high conversion rates—that is, build up the fraction of hits on the site that turn into purchases.
- Relationship-centered business models have high risk and potentially very high payoff; in contrast, transaction-centered business models are heavily reliant on price-cutting, discounts, and payments to portals.
- Relationship-centered business models succeed when they offer superb operational performance in fulfillment and reliability; transaction-centered business models, even when they perform superbly, remain vulnerable to online players who give away their service or goods to attract relationship business.
- Relationship-centered business models are creating new power brands; transaction-centered business models face loss of product equity to strong Internet relationship brand players.

These implications and differences are both dramatic and consequential to the entire success or failure of many Internet initiatives.

The relationship-versus-transaction distinction obviously points to very different business models. The same is true for the other value drivers hidden in Figure 1.1. If a firm can't see the deep patterns of what creates value, then its only real options in Internet planning are opportunism and reaction.

Opportunism comes from getting ahead of the change curve with some innovative idea, such as Priceline.com's reversing of pricing (from the seller sets the price to the customer sets the price). That can provide high payoff but at very high risk—it also rests on the soundness of the underlying business model; no firm can now preempt the market via just a Web site. The Web encourages opportunism, which translates to creativity. The barriers to entry are low; the willingness of investors to take high risks on an idea, start-up team, or technology remains high. Investors are increasingly looking for more than just concepts—and it can be hard to tell the difference between a creative idea and a dumb one.

Reaction comes from follow-the-leader. That's lower risk but lower payoff in almost all instances. The lack of barriers to entry for new Web players means that if your company is racing to copy an innovation, so too are plenty of others. As portals became the main game—if not in town then in industry, Netspeak, and the business press—and as business-to-business electronic commerce exploded in 1999, we saw a flood of companies racing to follow the leaders. Again, if all they are doing is trying to catch up to another firm or imitate it, this will be just another site among follow-the-leaders. At best, reaction gets a player back in the game. More typically, it leaves the company with no differentiation that offers value. It's six clicks down the AOL or Yahoo menu or a trailing result of a search engine request.

This last point is one that companies need to be very vigilant about. There are more and more indications that we are seeing the largest and fastest erosion of brand equity in business history. In the "six clicks down" example, AOL is the brand. With Priceline, when customers state the price they are willing to pay for an item, Priceline chooses the brand for them. In business-to-business trading hubs, many suppliers' brands will be lost—office supplies and commodity materials, for example. The implications of this shift are profound: a shift from product brand equity to relationship brand equity. We are already seeing in the revenue and repeat business growth of the Internet brand leaders how much this is worth.

Opportunism and reaction abound, thus clouding the picture even more for business managers. They create a flavor of the month and even a fashion show—what's in and what's out? Last year's Internet innovation soon becomes this year's conventional wisdom—a sort of e-truism—but by next year, it may well be recognized as incomplete or even wrong. For instance, an early .com e-truism was that the Web displaced bricks and mortar, with gurus forecasting the disappearance of retail stores, bank branches, and insurance offices. When that didn't happen, the e-truism became *clicks* and mortar: use the Internet to complement your existing channels and use your channels to complement the Internet. Blend those channels for success.

Charles Schwab ended debate about clicks *versus* mortar. Indeed it was a Schwab executive who first introduced the phrase "clicks and mortar."[5] Schwab is the discount broker that originally was bricks and mortar—sales branches—and telephones. It added clicks to become the Internet pacesetter in the securities business. In mid-January 2000, Schwab announced that it was adding a full-service firm to its online services, through an acquisition. So Schwab began with bricks, went to clicks and bricks, and is now buying more bricks. Meanwhile, it's overtaken most of the early clicks, like Ameritrade, and turned the top bricks players like Merrill Lynch upside down. Merrill Lynch, whose vice chairman publicly worried not so long ago that online trading could wreck the nation's financial safety, is going to clicks.

In 2000, the world moved on to mortar for clicks: companies whose core business was online started seeking out offline presence and partnerships. AOL and Yahoo made deals to be in Wal-Mart and Kmart stores, for example, and to give these retailers a presence on their electronic storefronts. More important, both the alliances explicitly aim at leveraging relationships with their own and each other's customers. While clicks retailers' sales grow, those that are the click offshoot of bricks often do better than expected. And as for the AOL merger with Time Warner, is that clicks and flicks?

This is all very volatile and confusing. There's so much going on that it's difficult for business managers to reach practical and reliable conclusions about what their firms should do. But there is a way to make sense of this and the many other dynamics of the Internet. Step back and ask what all the individual clicks, clicks versus mortar, clicks and mortar, and mortar for clicks companies tell us about general value drivers. The patterns really are there. For example, the winners harmonize all their channels on behalf of the customer. The losers get stuck talking about "channel conflict"—whether or not to bypass their existing distributors, or even to compete with them. Worse, like many of the established full-service commission security firms, they evaluate their own and online channels as alternatives, instead of a whole, viewing the situation as a Hamlet-like "To .com or not to .com, that is the question" dilemma.

A fundamental of Internet business is that the customer chooses. Clicks—the .com innovation—generated value to customers and revealed the limitations of purely online business. Smart firms took a look at where they could add value and remove limitations. Customers again responded, sending signals about their own value criteria. The brick firms started responding to that. The click firms began to see new opportunities in alliances with bricks. And in all this swirl of innovation and experiment, the picture is beginning to come clear.

Hidden within Figure 1.1—and revealed in Figure 1.2—are the general value driver patterns that we've uncovered after combing through many hundreds of examples. As you look at the companies in the top left-hand corner, for instance, what comes through consistently and pervasively is that their success or failure reflects relationship building, achieved through incentives and services that generate repeat business, personalization of the Web site and service, customization of offers, dynamic interaction with the customer, collaboration and focus on communities of interest to customer groups. Moving around Figure 1.2, we see a whole cluster of firms that have so leveraged logistics that they've changed the rules of supply chain management and operational efficiency, others that have transformed the very basics of capital deployment and payoff and of cost and margin structures.

There are six clusters of value drivers that explain just about everything we see happening in the Internet business space: logistics, relationships, channels, branding, capital and cost structures, and intermediation. This is not in any way a theory or "model" of Internet business. It's what's been happening since the Web took off, is happening now, and is the base for what firms are trying to make happen. The value drivers, not .com, are the base for long-term business success. That is, they're the signposts of the value path and the foundation of .profit.

IMPERATIVES FOR FUTURE VALUE AND PROFIT

We see value in Internet business—value for the customer and the company—as resting on a business model that responds to the value drivers. In other words, since value comes from these drivers, your business model has to feed into them and certainly not ignore them, or worse, conflict with them. From the six value drivers emerge the corresponding value imperatives—the management priorities for the business model.

Figure 1.2. The Value Drivers Shaping Success

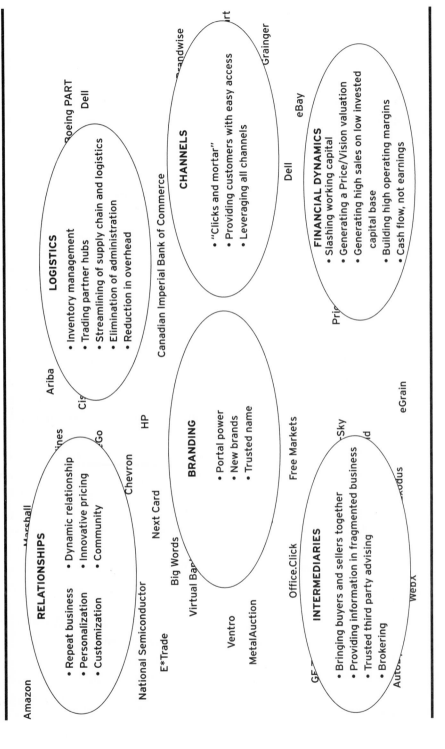

- *Perfect your logistics.* This imperative allows you to afford everything else—marketing, price reduction, service, and technology—and positions you to exploit the other opportunities of Internet business. Internet logistics along the external supply chain and internal process chain is now close to a requirement for being a well-run firm. Halving of inventories and of overhead is a very practical target. It's no exaggeration to say that any business model that ignores the Internet logistics imperative puts the company at risk. The evidence for this is now overwhelming; logistics leaders dominate the average players along every dimension of operations.

- *Cultivate your long-term customer relationships.* Nourishing your customer relationship is the only way to turn revenues into profits. Once you build a critical mass of repeat customers, add collaborators to your site, and cement relationship bonds via community, the margin advantage can be huge. If you focus only on the transaction without building the relationship base, all you have is huge marketing costs, price-based competition, and draining of financial capital. The fundamental reality of the Internet today is that the costs of customer acquisition are the equivalent of R&D for a high-tech firm—a major capital investment as the planned generator of value (though, like R&D, under accounting rules they are expensed). They are a claim on the future—a claim on value if they result in relationships that can be leveraged but a claim against revenues if they don't.

- *Harmonize your channels on behalf of the customer.* In general, a combination of the best of person-to-person, customer-to-call-center, and online interaction outperforms any one of these. Customers choose among the channels, each of which has its own special advantages for them and for you. Give them the choices that best build and maintain the relationship. Forget about channel conflict; customers see only channel choice. Forget about channel control; customers make their own choice.

- *Build a power brand.* The Internet is redefining the idea of brand. The new consumer power brands like AOL and Yahoo are *relationship* brands, not *product* ones. This changes the game. In the business-to-business area, start-ups have created brands as intermediaries that are in many instances stronger than most of the companies that use them (think of Ariba, FreeMarkets, and CommerceOne). In the business-to-consumer area, the consumers choose the winners: they determine the portals by making certain brands the cornerstone of their online relationship choices. Thousands of sites aim to become portals; customers choose just a few.

Those so chosen become cash flow machines with almost unlimited space to extend relationships, collaborations, and communities to influence services and providers. In effect, these brands-turned-portals are stars with gravitational pull affecting the orbit of many planets and their moons.

- *Transform your capital and cost structures.* In the longer term, .profit business is about the reversal of traditional views of balance sheets. All the items that are shown as financial assets on the left-hand side of the balance sheet are seen as what they really are—heavy economic and managerial liabilities that tie up capital and drain economic value added. The firms that move toward negative working capital and minimize the invested capital per unit of revenue and profit gain a Price/Vision premium in their market capitalization, which in itself so reduces their cost of capital that they play in an entirely different growth game from their competitors. Even when such firms are losing money as reported in their earnings statements, they are often *already* cash flow positive and generating very high revenues on very low invested capital; that's a platform for levels of .profit that offline firms, however strong their earnings, can't hope to match within their standard business models and economic structures. Underlying all the volatility of Internet company stock prices, the losses that many of them are piling up, and their cost of marketing is the drive to build the long-term .profit financial structure that firms such as Cisco, AOL, Dell, and Yahoo have already attained. In the end, this is the real Internet business "revolution."

- *Become a value-adding intermediary—or use one.* This slightly oddball imperative is largely complementary to the others. There's growing evidence that the next era of Internet business will be dominated by hubs: power brand portals and intermediaries. It will be they that control the interaction between suppliers and customers as dynamic brokers, information coordinators, trusted third-party advisers (value-adding intermediaries), and they that will be the places where customers choose to park on the Web (portals). Value-adding intermediation is niche-finding and niche-filling: through it, fragmented supply chains are linked and value roles are filled. This imperative moves in the opposite direction to most of the others, which is toward disintermediation. Everyone else will be a spoke into hubs. Business comes to the hubs. Spokes have to go and find that business—often by paying to be on the powerful portals.

These imperatives are illustrated briefly in Figure 1.3 and discussed at length in the chapters of Part Two.

Figure 1.3. The Business Model Value Imperatives

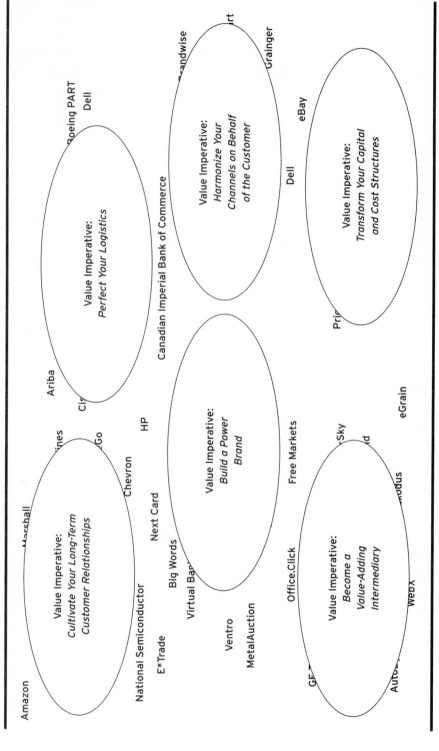

These value drivers and their imperatives are not business models per se—but they provide the templates for them and help you think through the following important problems:

- How well does your existing business model respond to these demands and opportunities?
- How sound are your Internet plans and operations in terms of their underlying implicit or explicit business model?
- What can and should your business model be?

Very roughly, most firms that are not yet factoring the Internet into their business vision and priorities and have only a limited Web presence need to be focusing on the first problem. The management question for them is, Are we in or out of the value game? Those that are more committed and active in the Web arena need to ask if they really do have a business model or are just in the .com mode of thinking. The third problem—What can and should our business model be?—is the one for companies to address in order to move along the value path toward .profit rather than just meander around the Internet marketspace.

All business models are unique—copycat strategies rarely work, as the .coms aiming to replicate Amazon, AOL, or Dell soon found out. Your own firm will place a different emphasis on each particular value imperative, depending on its ambitions, history, core competencies, target customer base. What we offer in *From .com to .profit* is not a dogmatic set of rules but useful and usable templates for building a business model for your circumstances—within a changing world. We offer a map and a compass—and our advice and illustrations as to how to use them. To find the right path for your company, your most direct route to .profit, you need these plus an overview of the landscape and a good sense of your goal.

THE EXECUTIVE CHALLENGE

Our goal in *From .com to .profit* is to provide business executives with clear pictures. One of the advantages of the .com approach to Internet business has been that it could be handled as technology by technology people. .Profit has to be handled as business and technology and by business people and technology people.

In general it is not being handled much at all. A study published in early 2000 by the accounting and consulting firm of Deloitte & Touche showed that 70 percent of retailers have no formal e-commerce strategy. "While roughly one third of retailers consider their online store to be strategic, a majority have set up Web operations with no clearly articulated strategy, and are merely testing the waters to gauge Internet demand."[6]

Another study of executives in nine industries found that 65 percent of management respondents viewed e-commerce as one of their most important initiatives but only 26 percent could point to one centralized decision maker in charge of it and less than half of these have control of the budget.[7]

Top executives are facing a huge challenge here. Barnes and Noble's CEO, Leonard Riggio—who for a decade was one of the most creative and outstanding innovators in American business—told the *New York Times* in an interview, "For the first time in my life, I can't see five years ahead the way I used to. . . . I can't see it clearly." He added, "It's not just the changes in the book business. It's the changes in retail, the changes in the way we live. I wake up and say that any business created before 1997 will be a fossil by the year 2010."[8]

In this context, business managers don't need to be told how important the Internet is nor do they need theories, forecasts, or techno-future scenarios. They most need pictures of the value path that will help them lead their organization to the new world of good business. That's the purpose of our book.

2

POSITIONING FOR THE .PROFIT ERA
GAINING THE BUSINESS MANAGEMENT ADVANTAGE

An "Internet strategy" is bad for your company's health.

The race to .com is well and truly over. We're climbing up the long and steep value path to .profit. To get there, managers must face facts: We're seeing the death of the transaction economy—a transaction isn't a relationship, and relationships, collaboration, and community are *everything* for the .profit era. Even the .com winners are having to show that they can turn their first mover advantage into a sustainable competitive and economic edge. Everything now rests on the firm's business model.

You need a business model to drive business strategy in the era of Internet-led business. A technology model can't drive business strategy and a technology strategy doesn't generate a business model. If you see the Internet as technology, you'll be stuck in .com thinking—looking for the right Web site design. Web sites don't create profit. The business model does.

It's in this sense that we say that an Internet strategy is bad for your company's health. An Internet strategy means that smart people are putting all their energy into answering the question, What do we do about the Internet? Not only is it the wrong question, but the answers far too often ignore business basics. The real question is, What do we do about our business basics in the Internet era? Then, the follow-on question addresses how to make use of Internet technology tools. Of course the firm must have first-rate Web design and operations and of course it needs to take advantage of all the astonishing new software, data management, and telecommunications tools that enable business expansion and innovation. But the end is business and the means is technology, not the other way around. As Wong Toon King, chairman of Silkroute Holdings Ltd., commented in early 2000 about the "market mania" in Asia, "Only one in 10 Internet startups will survive in the U.S., but I think it could be worse than one in 40 here in Asia. . . . There are far too many sites copying old ideas that do not bring anything new onto the Web."[1] Bear in mind that "old" here means at the longest five years.

Be warned: the established firms that got blindsided by .com players were often the best of their industry—Barnes and Noble, Compaq, Merrill Lynch, and Toys "R" Us. The success of these leaders' online rivals—Amazon, Dell, Schwab, and eToys—was not based on any competitive advantage in technology. Yes, they all used the Web—but anyone could have built the same Web sites as they did (or better). What they did was gain a business model edge that enabled them to leapfrog over some pretty smart companies. In the Internet economy, any company—even the best—is vulnerable to being blindsided in this way. And any company has the very same opportunity to do the blindsiding.

The stakes in the early phase of the .com era were tiny compared to the next phases of the Internet as part of the very basics of business, not an add-on or adjunct. To borrow from James Carville's reminder to the 1992 Clinton election team that "it's the economy, stupid!" executives need to realize that "it's the business model—and to ignore it is really, really stupid."

FROM VALUE IMPERATIVES TO BUSINESS MODEL

A business model is the basic blueprint for a company, into which it fits its Internet business priorities, strategic plans, and execution. The phrase is everywhere now—you can hardly find any issue of a business magazine or an Internet publication that doesn't use it somewhere. This is a very recent development. Previously, the articles would have used the word *strategy*. Business model has replaced strategy as the focus of discussion because strategy is defined within the givens of business—the givens of industry, customer base and behavior, channels, pricing and marketing. There are no givens now. To pursue a strategy and execute it superbly when it's based on a flawed business model is to be efficiently ineffective. .Profit rests on the business model. .Com rests on the Web site. It's common sense that if a company doesn't have a business model shaped around the drivers of value, then its Web site simply can't and won't ever move the company to .profit.

If a firm gets past .com and understands the value imperatives for .profit Internet business, it is then positioned to take the lead in handling this era of never-ending change instead of reactively trying to keep up and catch up. In Table 2.1, we present these value imperatives, the business basic that each relates to, and how each most contrasts with business as

Table 2.1. Value Imperatives in Action

Value Imperative	Business Basic	Previous Focus
Perfect your logistics	Operations and supply chain integration	Functional area administration Vendor management
Cultivate your long-term relationships	Customer relationship and interaction	Transactions Sales
Harmonize your channels on behalf of the customer	Channels and distribution	Channel control Web as single channel
Build a power brand	Branding and market positioning Portal power	Product brand equity
Transform your capital and cost structures	Corporate finance Investor relations Business valuation Capital Margins	Expense management P&L management P/E ratios
Become a value-adding intermediary	Market differentiation Intermediation	Industry positioning Industry definition

usual and hence with business model assumptions that, however well they may have applied before the Internet began reshaping the rules of the game, may now be obsolete.

At one level, this table has the appearance of just business common sense: logistics, customers, channels, brand, capital and cost structures, and value-adding roles. That's the point. If the value imperatives were not about business basics and a new common sense for a new era, then companies would not need to rethink their business models or look for new ones. The Internet would be what many business executives initially thought it was—an interesting but peripheral side issue, not relevant to the mainstream.

Imperative means "vital to do." This is not strategy; strategy is about how to do it. Imperatives imply an "or else" and an urgency. Here's our summary of why each value imperative is vital and urgent, plus what happens without attending to the imperative—the "or else":

Perfect your logistics because the leaders have shown that a company can transform its entire supply chain and related administrative processes to a degree that would have been unbelievable just five years ago. Or else: you won't be in the competitive game. You literally won't be able to afford to play.

Cultivate your long-term relationships because that is the only way to create the revenue base and margin base that makes you viable as the online economy becomes more and more the business mainstream. Or else: if you live only by the transaction, you will die by the transaction. There's no future in just transactions.

Harmonize your channels on behalf of the customer because customers are getting smarter and smarter about their options and about the pluses and minuses of online versus offline services, so that they shift their relationships to the best overall providers. Or else: you will be wrestling with channel conflict and losing any chance of being the best in distribution in a market where the leaders use every channel edge they can get—on behalf of the customer.

Build a power brand because you have to stand out in the relationship economy as a brand, not just one of thousands of Web sites with no differentiation in product, site, or price. Or else: you will be dependent on search engines and have to pay fees to branded portals.

Transform your capital and cost structures because this is the real revolution that's well under way, a revolution that changes the basics of balance sheets, cash flow, and shareholder value. Or else: goodbye.

Become a value-adding intermediary because this is how companies find differentiation by adding new value in the marketspace. Or else: you risk being disintermediated—bypassed by customers who migrate to hubs that add value for them.

The six imperatives overlap, of course, in leading companies' business models. Companies like Dell are exemplars in perfecting logistics, cultivating customer relationships, transforming capital and cost structures, *and* harmonizing channels, for example, and their success in each one of these feeds into the others. The skilled logistics company improves its capital and cost structures by reducing inventory (and hence working capital costs) and reducing overhead. The customer relationship winners similarly become so by paying careful attention to supply chain. So, the templates are not business plans or strategies. They offer blueprints and a way of learning from the best of the best. They aim at answering concerns like Leonard Riggio's (described in Chapter One) that, despite being CEO of a prosperous company, he could no longer clearly "see five years ahead."

That's a very, very different statement from "I don't know what our Internet strategy should be." But, in a way, they are equivalent. The clearer the CEO's understanding of the value imperatives and their business model opportunities and impacts, the clearer he or she will be about both company identity and Internet deployment.

In the .com era, it was for a while possible to make an impact in the market with a site that offered special information, special prices, or a broad catalog. But it will be harder and harder to find a sustainable differentiation; innovation is everywhere. It's now rare that any one player can keep so far ahead of the pack that it commands a Web site advantage.

Consider, for instance, the richness of business models, processes, channels, and relationships that are behind ten Web sites for buying cars that *PC Magazine* reviewed in March 2000.[2] Just two to three years before that, even a plain Web site offering information on cars, prices, and dealers was an innovation. Now, each of the companies must fight to differentiate itself and all of the following are part of everyday business:

- *American CarBuying Service:* Car-buying service for a fee, comparative lease quotes, negotiation of prices with dealers, handling of all paperwork, delivery of the car, consultants to help at all stages. *PC Magazine* rating: average.
- *AutoByTel:* Dealer referral service, comparison shopping, financing and insurance, auctions. Rating: very good.
- *CarOrder:* Research, customization of the car, pricing, ordering, and delivery without any contact with a dealer. Rating: excellent.
- *CarPrices:* Tutorials on purchase versus lease options, links to financing and insurance services, a choice of a guaranteed quote for a purchase or dealer bids. Rating: average.
- *CarsDirect:* Purchase, leasing, finance, insurance, delivery to your home or a dealer. Includes six years of roadside assistance. Rating: very good.
- *DriveOff:* Purchasing, financing, insurance, delivery tracking. Rating: very good.
- *MSN Carpoint:* The same plus in-depth research and comparison tools. Rating: very good.
- *Priceline Auto Service:* Option to specify the price you want to pay and how far you are willing to travel to pick up the car, guidance in making bids that are likely to be accepted by a dealer. No financing. Rating: very good.
- *StoneAge:* Locating the best price, auction service, help in applying for loans, leases, and insurance. Rating: Excellent.
- *UAutoBid:* Auctions: Dutch auctions, where the price drops until someone bids. Rating: average.

In this instance, the business models for the competing companies largely focus on channels—dealer relationships, financial intermediaries, and delivery mechanisms. They all also emphasize going beyond the car purchase transaction and aim at becoming the customer's personal agent. In other competitive arenas, the focus shifts to creating a lifetime customer relationship (financial service portals), to value-adding intermediation (business-to-business trading hubs), or to perfecting logistics (supply chain management hubs and services to customers via customized Web sites). But in all cases, they respond to the value imperatives of the online economy.

So, in looking ahead, how do you best prepare for an unknown future? Just as responding to industry deregulation isn't something the top management team assigns to the legal department, though of course it draws heavily on the legal department's inputs and expertise, responding to the Internet challenge and opportunity is not something it should delegate to the technology unit.

INTERNET: TECHNOLOGY OR MARKETING?

If the answer is the business model when the question is how to respond to the Internet value imperatives, then the key issue for the management agenda for action is who's in charge of getting to the answer. This isn't a technology issue any more. In our own work in companies, we've noticed that around half of all strategic Internet initiatives that are .profit-focused are led by the senior marketing executive. That reflects the firm's recognition of the value imperative of relationships. In others, it's very much a team of top managers creating a new strategic coalition, typically the chief operating officer in a manufacturing or distribution firm—the primacy here is logistics—plus the heads of information technology (IT) and marketing.

In the companies that are in .com mode, no one's really in charge of the business model. Maybe an outside Web design firm is brought in. Maybe the IT function spearheads Internet commerce pilot tests, sponsors intranets, and acts as an advocate for further initiatives. Maybe. This is "technology"—so it is seen as needing technical direction or, more often, it simply gets business management abdication. That in itself creates a competitive edge for the .com thinkers' competitors, old and new—they gain as the abdicators lose the business management advantage.

Historically, in most companies, responsibility for information technology strategy, oversight, and operations has rested with what is generally called the CIO—chief information officer. CIOs deal with technology architectures—the blueprints for the firm's IT platform. They are not in charge of its business blueprints; how could they be? That can leave a gap as the two blueprints converge because of the Internet. When electronic commerce meant *electronic* commerce, CIOs could best establish the direction for investing in technology and ensuring that it supported the company's priorities and operations. Continuing to do that doesn't work when it becomes EC. Worse, it is a major blockage in the move to eC, where it's the *commerce* that creates the value. Stated more bluntly, most firms don't have a business model for .profit and won't, because they don't see that the C must now drive the E.

The Internet is rapidly becoming the modern equivalent of electricity—a universal infrastructure that we never see, and that we take for granted and depend on in just about every element of our daily life. Electricity made possible entirely new ways of communicating (phone, fax), transformed customer relationships (try keeping a store open till 10 P.M. without electric lighting), lies behind many inventions (television, cars, photocopiers), enabled the average family to have the equivalent of dozens of household slaves (as you'll quickly recognize if your washing machine and dishwasher break down). Electricity is one of the main foundations of just about everything these days; it's simply an aspect of operations. But companies don't talk about their electricity strategy or assign a chief electricity officer. In the 1920s, Ford Motor Company did have a senior executive in charge of electricity strategy because this was technology and different from business as usual in an economy that had not yet seen the Tennessee Valley Authority transform the rural landscape of the United States or the grid standardize plugs, voltages, and transmission.

In February 2000, Ford announced that as part of its plan to be on the leading edge of technology and connect more closely with customers, it will provide computers, printers, and Internet usage at home for eligible employees—all at a nominal fee of $5 a month. As Chairman Bill Ford said, "Individuals and companies that want to be successful in the 21st century will need to be leaders in using the Internet and related technology."[3]

We're not yet at the point where the Internet is a foundation of just about everything—but nearly so, as Ford recognizes. Today, most firms feel they do need someone to be the modern-day equivalent of the chief electricity officer. But that will change. How soon is the issue. In the race to .com, your company at least had a clear goal—to build a Web presence in the exotic new info-, cyber-, e-, wired- space, market, society, community that began to take off in the mid-1990s. Here was this new wonder, the Internet—a combination of World Wide Web, browser, and personal computer that allowed anyone anywhere to buy, sell, communicate, publish, search, advertise, rent out space, or entertain. Anything you could think up, you could put on a Web site.

In 1996, this was rather like getting a cell phone. You didn't absolutely have to have one but it was neat and for some people soon became essential. By 1998, not having a Web presence was more like a company not having phones at all. In just two years, a new economic force had been built, most visibly by start-up firms whose entire identity was indicated by the .com in their name—Amazon.com, eBay.com, AutoByTel.com, Yahoo.com, and many others. Less obviously, but in many ways even more radically, established firms like Dell, Cisco, HP, and Charles Schwab added the Web to their customer relationship base, their channel management, and their logistics and supply chain management, and in doing so made a bundle of money and pushed many of their competitors into a sustained catch-up.

Business took over the Internet and began a rate of growth and expansion of breadth unseen before in history—in under four years. In the Christmas period of 1998, online purchases by consumers were double those for 1997. For Christmas 1999, they were up by a factor of four over the preceding year. Quite literally, electronic commerce was front page news. A reliable survey published by the University of Texas reported that the Internet economy amounted to $300 billion in 1997 and $500 billion in 1998, an almost 70 percent increase.[4] Box 2.1 shows some of the business news of 1999 about the Internet; it's obvious from just these examples that we really do have a new Internet *economy*.

And, of course, 2000 continued the flood of business news with the announcement in early January of the planned AOL–Time Warner merger, likely to be seen as one of the pivotal dates in Internet business history. If the 1995 foundation of Amazon and launch of Netscape marks the start of the .com race, this was when the distinction between the "old" and "new" economy blurred. The key issue for 1999 was the idea of the Internet *as* business. In 2000 that was already passé—the key issue was Internet *in* business.

This isn't a "new" economy anymore and it certainly isn't a "bubble" economy, and it's not something to be handled as electricity in the 1920s.

Box 2.1. A Sampling of 1999's Business Events and Impacts

- Banc One launches its independent Internet bank, Wingspan, which offers much better deals than its own well-established parent: around 12 percent higher interest on certificates of deposit, for instance—5.7 percent versus 4.97 percent.

- Japan announces the full deregulation of securities commissions: on September 30, 1999, the commission for the purchase of 1 million yen ($9,000) of stocks was $105. On October 1, it was $22 via the online trading company E*Trade Japan and $6 via Monex, a start-up Japanese Internet player, partly funded by Sony.

- Merrill Lynch, whose vice chairman in mid-1998 described online securities trading as a danger to U.S. financial health, announces its own online venture.

- Internet trading accounts for 60 percent of Charles Schwab's revenues.

- America Online is generating close to a billion dollars a quarter of free cash flow. Its advertising revenues for Quarter 2 are over $300 million, with a backlog of $1.5 billion. Revenues for 1999 were $4.8 billion, with profits of $396 million. The figures for 1992 were $26.6 million sales and $3.5 million profits.

- Dell reaches the $30 million level of daily sales, up from $1 million in 1997. Its return on invested capital is well over 200 percent.

- Federal Express handles 70 percent of all customer transactions and queries via the Web; its goal is 100 percent. The average saving is $10 a query—for 60 million messages per day.

- Of Cisco's more than $6 billion of orders made over its online Internet service, 80 percent are never handled by the company, nor does it ever take delivery of the parts or finished goods. Online links to foreign contract manufacturers, third-party logistics firms, and other collaborators deal with this virtual inventory.

- Amazon's run rate—its annualized rate of sales—reaches $2 billion; this is the equivalent of building around 150 superstores.

- The following companies are all generating revenues of over $1 billion a year related to the Web: Dell, Cisco, IBM, Ingrams, UPS, American Airlines, Schwab, Amazon, Hewlett-Packard, America Online.

TECHNOLOGY IN CONTEXT:
ENABLING BUSINESS MODELS FOR TOMORROW

All this adds up to an irreversible transition from the Web site as the focus of planning and investment—.com—to following the value path to .profit with the business model as the navigation aid. But in no way does this mean that technology does not matter, only that it has to be viewed in terms of value imperatives. It's outside the scope of our book to go into detail about what's happening today in innovations in software, hardware, data management, and telecommunications tools, but every major development entirely supports, enhances, and extends the value imperatives.

The technology of the .com era in itself enabled business models that would have been fantasies without it, just as in the 1960s placing a bank branch inside a 7-11, on the street corner, or in a hotel lobby and keeping it open every day, all day, would have been an impractical daydream. The cost, speed, and availability of telecommunications of the late 1970s turned dream into the ATM as innovation and then part of everyday routine. In the same way, the combination of the World Wide Web, Web browser, personal computer, and Internet Service Provider did the same—dream to invention to innovation to everyday service.

From the vantage point of four years on, this toolkit looks almost antique. There's been an accelerating extension from storefront and "site" to more and more customization and personalization. In addition, the technology and its uses are rapidly becoming more and more dynamic. The new generation of software shifts opportunities from the relatively static storefront provided by the basic .com toolkit to whatever personalized, customized, and interactive "e-services"—Hewlett-Packard's term for the new value-generating Web offers—that you can envisage. Box 2.2 presents a simple consumer example.

As we go to press, the scenario in the box does not yet play out, but it will very soon—well within two years at the outside. New technology such as HP's e-speak software platform enables it, the business forces underlying the path to .profit—value for customers via new and personalized services—demand it, and the American Automobile Association (AAA) is already working on it through its Response Center Services. Far from

Box 2.2. Roadside Service, Internet Style

Your car breaks down on a business trip. You are around ten miles from the nearest town and you are unfamiliar with the area. You will be late for your meetings and will almost certainly miss your plane. What do you do?

Because of technology, we're long since past the point at which you either had to fix the car yourself, wait for a friendly motorist to help out, or trek to a highway call box. Chances are that you have a pager or a cellular phone with you in the car and so can begin the process of getting help and calling ahead to change your appointments. But even with these conveniences, you do the calling and you do the work. If, for instance, you have a wireless digital phone with Internet access (widely available in Europe and now hitting the United States), you can log on to the Net and search for sites that can handle your problem. In varying degrees, today's technology has helped your flexibility but it still requires that you refocus your efforts and change your day dramatically. But take a step to the immediate future and what do you do?

You don't do anything. Your car is an Internet address. We expect that to be standard by 2002 at the latest. Already in 2000 General Motors is the largest seller of microprocessors in the world with its larger cars containing around $3,000 worth of chips. Any device can and will be an Internet Protocol (IP) address; today, that already includes cell phones, printers, refrigerators, and cameras. Of course, your car has a Global Positioning System (GPS) in it—it can access the satellite-based service that

science fiction, this small scenario is *completely* practical within today's technology base—once that base is fully rolled out. It doesn't depend on any breakthroughs; there's no need for a computer to understand what you say or for any radical new wireless tools, telecommunications, or software. It demands a lot of engineering (today's digital wireless networks have many inadequacies) and it will be awhile before we have high-speed and reliable coverage for Internet phone communications. It will also take time to build the base of electronically linked service providers and for customers to adopt the idea. As with online ordering of groceries for home delivery, it may take years of marketing to attract a critical mass of cus-

pinpoints your location anywhere in the world within a few feet, and it has a wireless IP link of its own and can act on your behalf.

The car's software has already diagnosed that the breakdown is a failure in the ignition system. It now broadcasts a request across the Internet to qualified local service stations and parts suppliers for bids to handle your problem, including coming out to pick you and your car up and make the repair. Given the urgency of your timetable, as indicated by your calendar, which a separate App-on-Tap (the term for the new generation of Internet software that provides services on demand via the Web) accesses, another message is getting you the best offer on a rental car.

Meanwhile, the car manufacturer's database systems are being updated about the failure of the component. Since this is the twelfth similar occurrence in the past two weeks, an alert is sent to the engineering and quality control departments.

Also, in the background and as a matter of routine, the people you were due to meet are automatically being e-mailed or paged about your delay. And your flight is being rebooked through a software module that invites online travel service providers to bid for the best combination of price and schedule, as per the profile and preferences you had already specified on your personal Web site. Minutes after your car comes to a stop, the dashboard display lights up with a list of arrangements for your approval.

---

tomers, more years to get rid of all the glitches, and perhaps even more to start making money.

That said, this is all fully feasible and the overall scenario it lays out is inevitable, as shown in Box 2.3. It's inevitable because it fits into the dominant trend of Internet business: relationships via services. The business model underlying our example has as its priorities customization and personalization in those relationships via collaboration. The service is customized to you, your schedule, your situation, and even your individual car. The service provider acts as a broker through collaborative interactions with other providers.

Box 2.3. The Online Caddy

During a demonstration at the 1999 Specialty Equipment Market's annual meeting, a driver of a Cadillac Seville was able to use the following services provided by the General Motors OnStar service:

- Have traffic data, stock quotes, and an e-mail message read aloud by a computerized voice
- Play a song sent via the Internet to the car as an MP3 sound file
- Test out other OnStar services—getting directions, tracking a stolen car, and calling an ambulance if the air bag deploys
- As of the end of 1999, OnStar had around a hundred thousand subscribers at a cost of $17 a month for basic service and $33 for premium service.[5]

Our examples relate to consumer services. For business relationships and collaborations, we are already seeing electronic brokers and software agents that act automatically to update partners in a supply chain, bid on your firm's behalf in an auction, monitor shipping rates, and so on—any service that can be embodied in software. This is a new generation of software and telecommunications tools and the first to be explicitly designed for the world of the Internet. Hewlett-Packard's e-speak software platform, which we discuss briefly in Chapter Eleven, is setting the pace. It enables new types of conversation and brokering between new types of devices and will, in turn, enable new business models.

BOLTING TOWARD PRODUCTIVITY— THROUGH THE PORTAL

The new e-services dynamic can be seen in action today, not in your car, but in many Internet innovations in business-to-business Internet relationships. One example is VerticalNet, which creates trading hubs for over forty business communities that include solid waste management specialists and makers of food ingredients, adhesives, and paints. Its criteria for setting up a portal to link buyers, sellers, and trading partners are that an industry must contain at least three thousand companies and that those companies must have forty thousand buyers and a total of $10 billion in sales. For $6,000 per player per year, less than a mailshot promotion, VerticalNet hosts what is in effect a massive market of company storefronts, passing on sales leads, managing auctions, creating new sales avenues, bringing communities together on line for news, promotions, and so on. It creates major opportunities for companies to sell in areas where they have no sales force. For example, 40 percent of VerticalNet's traffic is now international, with companies reporting sales orders from countries in which they have no presence whatsoever.

VerticalNet is creating marketplaces; creating communities; inventing new modes of transaction, selling, and trading; and growing its own long-term relationship base. Its record is impressive: it has a 90 percent renewal rate. VerticalNet is still a tiny company in terms of revenues and number of employees but what it is doing is as different from the standard procurement Web site as that itself was from the physical site it substituted for.

This is all a very new style of doing business. It *invents* value for a wide community of players who previously operated very much as "suppliers," "buyers," "distributors," and brokers. Now, they form a collaborative marketspace via the VerticalNet portals and hubs. It is this focus on value that shifts attention from the .com to services and to the customer relationships, collaborations, alliances, acquisitions, and marketing offers that turn the site into something so new that we've lacked any words for it. These are new brands, new middleman players in supply chains, new online equivalents of airport hubs, gateways, junction boxes, and channel killers—new "somethings." *Portal* has become the general term to describe these strange new creations. Some even use entirely newly coined terms like *vortal* (for vertical portal), net market maker, functional hub, or butterfly market.

Whatever they are named, these new somethings emerge as coordination points for supply chain partners, reducing all players' costs and increasing their shared information and communication flows. An early example is General Electric's Trading Partner Network (TPN), which saves GE up to 15 percent on supplier prices and is the base for Sony to leverage its distributor chain and for Fruit of the Loom to provide free Web sites to its own distributors to strengthen their operations and reinforce the company's own branding and supply chain management. Pick up any Internet business periodical and you'll find at least a dozen examples a month.

They destroy industry categories. (For example, what "industry" is Amazon in? What about America Online?) They build very large revenue bases—and for some, very large cash flows—with massive productivity rates. According to *Business 2.0*, the average U.S. company generates $160,000 of revenues per employee; the figure for Internet companies is 65 percent higher—on average.[6] Here are just a few other examples of Internet businesses with sales in excess of $100 million a year and far above-average business-generation productivity: E*Trade generates $415 thousand in revenues per employee; eBay, $546 thousand; CD Now, $627 thousand; Cyberian Outpost, $981 thousand; and Preview Travel, $1 *million*.[7]

Think of how long it would take to build a $1 billion business from scratch in the old style, and all the investment, planning, time, and organization that it would take to develop all the standard functional areas, processes, head count, equipment, offices, training, reporting relationships, and the like. Instead, most of today's high productivity companies are bolted together electronically, not built organizationally. Billion-dollar portals use a new generation of software to link to masses of other companies in effect to rent, borrow, or pay for these capabilities as needed and are "large" firms within a year or two of starting their operations. If they need shipping and logistics, they might link to UPS—and never even see the goods. Credit financing? Another application program interface (API) to eCredit.com. The procurement department? It's in the customized Web site provided by Cisco or built by Ariba. Want more business going through the site? Add links, ads, sponsorships, orders, to and from just about anything from anyone from anywhere.

This ability to substitute electronic external links for internal operations and do so on the fly—no waiting, and with everything happening automatically—shifts the nature of online business itself. The shift is away from the Web site as a sort of storefront to a company as a complex of services within a complex of marketplaces. It's more than just a sprint to .com; it's a long distance race to a whole new way of business.

THE NEW RACE: GORILLAS IN OUR MIDST

The most widely cited winners that have emerged from the .com era are Amazon, Dell, and Cisco. Think of these Big Three as the gorillas in their ecosystem—this is Geoffrey Moore's insightful term, and it captures the dynamics of competition in high-tech markets and the Internet.[8] Gorillas dominate a hypergrowth territory, piling up so many advantages that their market valuation soars while their cost of capital remains low.

Amazon is already a mature company, as vulnerable to new modes of competition as it made the established bookstore chains vulnerable to an entirely new business model. Dell is the equivalent in logistics of Toyota; Toyota set the agenda for three decades for manufacturing through its leadership of just-in-time, lean production, and total quality management. Dell has done the same in the personal computer retailing business. But it, too, faces challengers with new business models, most notably the manufacturers and retailers that are using massive price discounts and free offers to attract buyers of low-end PCs. For now, Cisco's gorilla advantage is such that it was able to spend almost $7 billion for a company (Cerent) in stock at a total cost of just over 3 percent of its equity base.[9] Cisco as yet hasn't seen much challenge to its spot in the telecommunications equipment ecosystem but that challenge will come.

Although the first gorillas in Internet business did not make any major innovations in technology, they didn't stick with the core technology either. Amazon brought a new way of thinking about online customer relationships, distribution, cost structures, and branding—and used the Internet technology available to every firm. Dell brought its established skills in customer service via call centers, business process streamlining, supply chain management, and management of financial capital—and used the widely available core Internet technology. Cisco did the same, bringing a business model that emphasizes aggressive innovation via the acquisition of the technology and skills it needs to maintain its leadership.

Each of the gorillas is a leader in using the emerging tools of e-services, all of which are becoming available to every player. Somewhere out there are plenty of new companies who will exploit e-services technology and business smarts the way Amazon, Dell, and Cisco exploited standard Web technology—and that have the superb business smarts and ability to execute their invasion of the territory. Indeed, the .profit game is already seeing plenty of baby gorillas—potential winners. These are the fast-growth companies that bring compelling business models to the gorilla game. Many of these, perhaps most, also benefit from the e-services technology base in ways that the .com firms could not.

First to the Web is no longer the advantage. There are plenty of baby gorillas, some recent entrants, some Fortune 1000 companies, some yet to be born. They will bring an effective new business model to the game, raise the capital to feed themselves till they are big enough to roam the wilds at will—and use the new widely available technology. These days, it's all much more a matter of first-to-the-portal, supply chain hub, customer relationship niche, and business process edge. That combination won't necessarily come from a start-up any more than it did in the .com phase. Because Amazon stands out as one of the successes of Internet history, and because Dell and Cisco have so dominated their business territories, it's easy to associate Internet success with Startup-Company.com. But Dell and Cisco were already major successes and well established as leaders in revenue and profit growth, innovation, and customer service. America Online predated the first phases of the Internet by a decade and is just as much a gorilla as Yahoo, a start-up firm with a similar business model.

Managers should never assume that it will be new companies that continue to set the pace. Instead, it will be *any* company that gets the management combination right. The points we make in this chapter are simple: everything follows from business managers' taking charge of the business model as their own responsibility. If they don't, then .com becomes by default the business model in action, regardless of whether or not it addresses the value imperatives of Internet business.

MAKING THE MANAGEMENT DIFFERENCE

"It's the economy, stupid." We could extend James Carville's remark and say about the Internet that now "it's the economy." We won't add "stupid" because to do so would trivialize the issue managers are facing. They are not stupid when they don't quite know how to respond to the challenges and opportunities of the Web-as-business world. There's never in history been a force that so affects just about every aspect of business and society at such a pace. The Industrial Revolution took over a hundred years to transform the world. That makes the speed of the Web revolution all the more astonishing. It's not even a decade old and even though it constitutes only 1–2 percent of overall business revenues it's transformed the basics. How then can anyone easily make sense of what's happening and confidently plan ahead? Yes, it's the economy and no, you're not stupid.

But it will be stupid for executives not to take charge of their company's future in this economy. That's why it's the business model that counts. In some ways that's a fancy term for being clear about the basics of the business direction. It's highly pragmatic and provides a picture of the future. We, the authors of *From .com to .profit,* have lived in the world of information technology for decades and have been at the very center of the Internet business world, in our roles as manager, researcher, writer, consultant, and educator. So we've been where all the "new" is in this economy, with its dazzle, pace, surprises, explosions, and roller-coaster rides. But the more we move with the new, the more clear it is to us that what lies below the surface of technology matters most: the business basics that lead to value creation that provides for a business model opportunity.

And it's these that managers should focus on in taking charge of change instead of reacting to it. Our strong recommendation is that managers take our list of value imperatives and ask how clear is the picture that they, their planners, their key line managers, and their staff have about the value path to .profit. They need a picture of what the firm will be like two to five years out in terms of each of the imperatives. A missing or cloudy picture is a major warning signal. Here are the pictures managers need to sketch out. Filling them out in more detail builds the business model. Get the sketch first. It will clarify everything:

- *Logistics:* Where, why, and how does our picture of our near future show us exploiting all the now-proven opportunities the Internet provides in supply chain management, operations, and coordination of logistical processes?
- *Relationships:* Who are our customers of tomorrow and why are we confident they will stay with us and grow their business with us?

- *Channels:* What's the customers' experience going to be in how they deal with us and how we deliver to them? What do we do ourselves and what do distribution partners do for us and for the customers for all our mutual benefit?
- *Capital and costs:* What will our balance sheet and income statement look like when we get through the investment phase of our commitment to the value path to .profit?
- *Branding:* What's our identity in this new economy? How will we stand out from the pack?
- *Value-adding intermediation:* Where do we become indispensable to customers and business partners?

That's the agenda for today to make a management difference for tomorrow.

3

DELIVER VALUE TO CUSTOMERS AND PROFIT FOR THE FIRM THROUGH RELATIONSHIP, COLLABORATION, AND COMMUNITY

Forget "first mover advantage." Today's rule: Build relationships, collaborate, reach communities–or die.

So far in *From .com to .profit*, we've focused on the move from .com to generating value from a Web presence. But where does that value come from? Internet business really is profitable—but only if your firm understands the critical economic link between relationships, collaboration, and community as customer value and their impact on capital and margins. Without value for customers there will be no profit: value has to precede profit. But profit is very much the issue—how to finish off the move and get from value to .profit. Many companies are creating massive value but with no sign they will ever be profitable. It's all too easy to go broke through value: spend an average of $200 per new customer on marketing, offer a $50 rebate deal to new customers, cut prices by 15 percent, pay AOL and similar portals a fee for referrals, give away free trades, free Internet sites, free shipping. You can expect plenty of business. But profit? Alas, no.

The key to .profit is exactly the same as the key to creating value: relationships, not transactions. Firms build relationships through repeat business; that changes their cost structures and begins to recover the massive costs of customer acquisition. They extend relationships through collaborations that add services via links to other online companies. That also changes their cost structures: it enables them to build more business without investing extra capital. They strengthen the relationships even more through community building: providing a coordination and communication hub for shared interest groups, professional communities, and logistics partners. That generates cost and revenue opportunities through networks of relationships and collaboration.

Relationships, collaboration, and community: these underlie just about every aspect of the Internet, not just Internet business. For business, they underlie just about every aspect of turning value into profit.

THE ECONOMIC REALITIES OF INTERNET BUSINESS

Internet business demands masses of investment: $200 million to build a customer base of a million, $5 million in first-year marketing for a portal presence, $50 million for a five-year contract with a portal, $150 million to upgrade a retailing or trading network.[1] These are typical for a large-scale venture, not exceptions at all. The expenditures aren't repaid by building revenues—it's the margins on those revenues that count. It's hard to know how to turn Internet revenues into margins, because today most Internet companies are flamboyant loss makers. It's even harder to compete online when at the very same time as you are building the customer and revenue base, you have to build up your cost base and pour out money for marketing, slash prices, and pay for new technology infrastructures.

This is why Internet companies look so unprofitable. Marketing and infrastructure building are largely expensed under IRS rules and generally accepted accounting principles. But they are really capital, exactly the equivalent of R&D, which is also expensed. Intel pours money into R&D today to position itself for tomorrow. Internet firms do the same with their marketing costs. If Intel were to slash its investment in new chip design, its reported earnings would soar—but surely its stock price would plummet. Of course, if the magic flow of innovations were to slow for a lengthy period of time, then and only then would its stock price increase if it cut back on its R&D.

Internet players' investments in marketing and infrastructure follow very much the same dynamics. They are the capital investment today that generates tomorrow's value. As long as investors see the value path, they'll bid up the company's valuation. As many commentators have pointed out, Amazon, which spends over 20 percent of its revenues on marketing— more than it spends on technology—could become "profitable" in the accounting sense of the term in six months or so; all it has to do is stop spending money on marketing. Would it be a stronger company if it did this? The jury is out. Just as many commentators completely dismiss its chances of recovering the stream of investment capital it is spending as believe that its business model will succeed. (We're cautious believers.)

Ironically, it may be in Amazon's and other expanding firm's interests that marketing costs are an expense. If it were able to capitalize them, it would become profitable earlier than it would otherwise be under existing accounting rules. But that would mean it would pay taxes on those profits. Instead, it's able to retain the cash flow surplus from its operations.

As Cern Basher, vice president of Provident Investment Advisers, commented in March 2000, the accounting system we use today was designed over five hundred years ago (by an Italian mathematician named Luca Paoli) to keep track of transactions through the principle of double entry bookkeeping, where each revenue item is credited to an account and the corresponding expenses debited. He quotes Baruch Lev, professor of accounting at New York University's Stern School of Business, who is a highly influential critic of the limitations of account systems in handling intellectual capital and intangible assets, of which Internet marketing investments are a major and growing factor in the economy: "The problem with intangible assets is that they are very expensive to both acquire and to develop, they're extremely difficult to manage, and when you are building a knowledge asset, you could quite possibly end up with nothing. . . . Accounting records transactions, but much of value creation or value destruction precedes any transaction." He singles out AOL's expensing of its customer acquisition costs during its period of "tremendous growth" as an instance of the mismatching and disconnect between accounting records and business value and states that it's a problem that will be very hard to solve in terms of both theory and practice, so we will have to live with the systems we now have.[2]

Our focus is on business management rather than the details of financial accounting per se, but we see the issue of financial structures as central to effective management planning for .profit. So, our strong recommendation is that *from a business model planning perspective,* you view customer acquisition as capital, view costs in terms of their dynamics rather than static numbers—that is, look at how they are affected by growth and how they can be improved by following the value imperatives—and view profitability in terms of real cash flows.

Basically, a .profit-focused company is betting that it can build repeat business that provides very high margins (eBay), good margins on very high volumes (Dell), or no margins on its own transactions but excellent profits from fees as a portal hosting others and from advertising (Yahoo, AOL), or from fees as a broker, auctioneer, or supply chain hub (Ariba, Chemdex, FreeMarkets, and many others). The bet requires it to come into the game with a lot of up-front money that it will spend on attracting and serving customers. These marketing, technology, customer fulfillment, shipping, and other support costs won't begin to be recovered by even very high-volume transactions. The profits will come from a combination of ensuring repeat business, using (or becoming) portals, and bonding customer relationships.

Ensuring Repeat Business

Whereas the initial "buy" transaction for a new customer generally is a loss, the margins on a stream of follow-on online orders can be spectacular. The reported incremental margin, excluding allocated marketing and infrastructure costs, for eBay, Ariba, Yahoo, Schwab, and others is 50–80 percent. It's not considered unusual. Amazon is absorbing massive losses on initial business now in order to benefit from its 70 percent repeat business rate. The repeat business figure for its offline competitors is in single figures: the book industry operates with net margins of 3–5 percent.

Incremental margins on digital products and services are naturally much higher than for physical goods and location- and people-dependent services, because electronic transaction handling costs pennies or even fractions of a penny. That's why eBay's operating margin—less, of course, its investments in expanding its infrastructure base—has routinely been 70–85 percent.

One of the long-term consequences of this, which is in itself a threat to product brand equity, is that a strong branded portal or hub may well be able to sell your product cheaper than you can. It will be a branded broker taking a small fee that earns it more margin than the manufacturer.

Using (or Becoming) a Portal

A successful portal draws in customers and keeps them happy, making them more and more open to trying out new offers from it and from other companies highlighted on it. Thus companies looking for .profit need to buy a presence on a portal or establish one of their own. This gives established portals substantial leverage in the marketplace. For a sense of what AOL has become, consider that drkoop.com (established in 1999 by well-respected ex-Surgeon General Everett Koop) agreed to pay AOL $89 million over five years for a preferred position on the site. (In April 2000, drkoop.com announced it was running out of cash and renegotiated the deal, with AOL getting an equity position.) AOL is now like a CBS or an ABC: it makes money from ads when giving its programs away free to viewers. And when a portal like Yahoo has 100 million subscribers, it owns a franchise that, not surprisingly, is generating almost a 90 percent renewal rate from the close to two thousand companies that advertise on it.

Bonding the Relationship

Bonding the customer relationship via personalization, customization, and customer self-management is key. Here's an extract from an ad that announced MySchwab back in 1999:

> Using award-winning customization software from Excite.com, MySchwab allows you to build your own home page, putting the tools you need to help keep track of your finances in one convenient place.[3]

That's pretty bland—it's not the real news here. The illustration in the ad lists "the tools you need" as Financial Planning, Stock Quotes, Live Investment Forums, and Mutual Fund Help. That all makes sense for a financial service company, but there's more. How about Sports Scores and News, Weather, and personal news feeds and alerts? Adding them makes plenty of sense—if you think long-term relationships and not just securities trading transactions.

MySchwab is illustrative of many other consumer and business portals that are hitting on all the customer relationship cylinders. The more that customers *routinely* go to the site and the more they value it for the full range of offers it provides, the larger the volumes at high incremental margins—again, if and only if the initial marketing and infrastructure investment has been recovered. So financial planning creates selling opportunities as it builds the ongoing interaction between customer and Schwab. Live investment forums build new communities of shared interest: community has always been the single most powerful force on the Web. AOL's chat rooms built its customer base, which was closing in on a billion messages as 2000 approached. A 1999 Nielsen survey showed that people spend three times longer at their MyXYZ home portal than at the competing sites that provide the same services and information.

To reach .profit—and even to survive today—you simply can't go it alone. You need partners everywhere. Sports scores and news link Schwab to collaborators, many of whom pay a fee for this but also gain from the association.

THE ECONOMICS OF VALUE—TOWARD .PROFIT

Just what are the economics of .profit companies? Consider a set of hypotheticals, one traditional and three Internet companies. In the first diagram (Fig. 3.1), our hypothetical company, Landlocked, has a lower fixed cost structure than any of the other three. Because it has higher variable costs—labor, stores, distribution channels, and so on—it has lower margins. If Landlocked operates at, say, 10 percent above breakeven it does not make much money—but if it falls 10 percent below, it doesn't lose much money on operations, either.

Dreamboat (Fig. 3.2) is in a very different situation. At 10 percent below breakeven, it is losing its own or its investors' capital at staggering rates, because it is spending so much on marketing, technology, and service support.

We call the company Dreamboat as a reminder that it may be on a trip to Fantasy Island and that the dream may turn out to be an illusion. But look at Dreamboat's upside margins once it's above breakeven. It probably won't sustain those, but instead will slash prices, increase volumes, and sustain relationships. Then it looks like the third diagram (Fig. 3.3), where it's now Dreambucks.

Figure 3.1. Landlocked

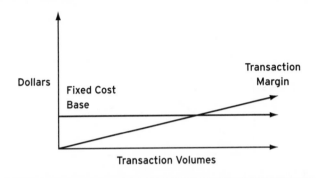

Note: This is a typical bricks-and-mortar firm—its gross operating margins are around 5 percent manufacturing and 12 percent services. With variable costs high and fixed costs low, it won't make or lose much money if beyond 10 percent above or below breakeven.

Figure 3.2. Dreamboat

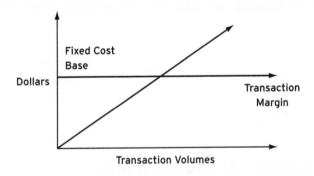

Note: This is an aspiring Internet Gorilla—it takes on heavy fixed costs for marketing, infrastructure, and support, and it generates good margins from incremental transactions. It must build relationship business and benefit from the cost advantage of online operations. At 10 percent below breakeven, it looks like a disaster, but investors are funding the gamble.

Figure 3.3. Dreambucks

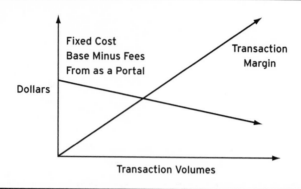

Note: This is the Internet ideal—portal fees (ads, hosting) offset fixed cost investment, and fixed marketing costs drop as brand and relationships strengthen. It can grow volumes dramatically by giving away margin and cutting prices.

The fourth hypothetical is Sinkingship (Fig. 3.4), with massive fixed costs and eroding margins. It has high marketing costs and selling, general, and administrative expenses, a poor supply chain, and weak relationships with its customers.

Effective cost structures are the key to the earnings side of .profit. It's that simple in concept. It's not so easy in practice, of course. But again, the very same foundations that underlie the relationship aspects of Internet value drivers fuel their economic ones, too. Collaboration is a business growth imperative.

FUTURE GROWTH: RELATIONSHIP, COLLABORATION, AND COMMUNITY REQUIRED

There are three basic truths about the Internet economy.

- Everything about the Web is now personal—that's what *relationship* means, as opposed to *transaction*. If you try to live by the transaction— a product sell—you'll die by it.
- You simply can't go it alone in terms of either technology or business. You must collaborate with customers, other service and product providers, technology providers, and even competitors. You're only as strong as your weakest ally.

Figure 3.4. Sinkingship

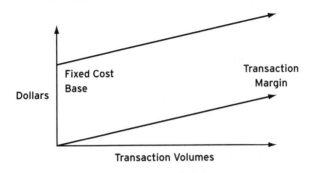

Note: This is an Internet Chapter 11 company—the worst of both offline and online worlds. Marketing costs and infrastructure investments keep going up to attract customers, but transactions don't generate relationship margins and profitability. Capital dries up as investors bid the stock down and down; there's no money for expansion, so the site cuts prices and margins drop.

- Abstractions like consumers, demographics, and even markets disappear in this world of relationship and collaboration. In the consumer marketplace, there is nothing more personal than the Web and nothing so powerful on it as the pull of communities, from chat rooms to sites customized to a company, profession, or interest group.

This is a lesson most obvious in the somewhat surprising success of America Online, which reached a zenith in its merger with Time Warner, a company three times as large as itself in terms of revenue, but very much the junior partner in terms of the financial agreement. AOL's demise has been predicted many times in its almost twenty-year history (which predates the Internet): poor technology, threats from other online service companies (now largely defunct or acquired by AOL), threats from the Net itself as making AOL unneeded, and threats from poor customer service. Now that America Online is a money machine, it's easy to forget how long it took the company to become profitable and why it was able to do so.

AOL spent around half a billion dollars on distributing free software disks with up to a hundred hours of free initial service. Many new customers used the free time and then dropped the service. It won in the end because of its community focus. Its chat rooms attracted many people with shared interests (our personal favorite is the "Vultures as Pets" room). Its simple-to-use electronic mail service encouraged the search for long-lost friends and bonded families scattered across the country or even the world.

In the business-to-business market, community has become the base for a new style of personalization: facilitating, enabling, and even creating communities online. When a firm puts together the three forces of relationships, collaboration, and community, it plays a different game from other online players and leverages the strengths of the e-services approach.

National Semiconductor: Targeting—and Redefining—the Customer

A fairly typical example of a success in targeting the customer is National Semiconductor.[4] Originally, when it opened up its Web site for customers to place orders for computer chips, it assumed that "customer" meant procurement agent, the person who made the purchase transaction. Over time, it saw that agents formed just one of its customer communities. Within two years of its launch, National Semi's Web site was drawing half a million customer design engineers who access it for the latest information on computer chips.

National Semi targeted the site to the customers at the very front end of the buying chain: the engineers who do the technical evaluation of the components that will be built into their companies' products, such as cell phones. It has carefully and comprehensively linked the Web site to the internal business; sales leads flow from it directly into the firm's opportunity management system and all customer e-mail messages are answered by the National Semi employees to whom they are routed. That may be any one of eight thousand (out of a total of nineteen thousand). Employees receive a daily set of charts reporting data from the Web site, such as what products customers are interested in and what samples they asked for. (By contrast, surveys routinely show that around 85 percent of companies either don't accept e-mail from customers or don't reply—so much for relationship and collaboration.[5])

Next National Semi segmented purchasing agents, buyers, and component engineers, all of whom have very different relationship interface needs and value drivers. The National Semi Purchasing Resource Web site was developed to accommodate these. Purchasing agents need fast delivery of small quantities of components when their engineers are in the design stage for a new product. The site links them to the order end systems of distributors who have the item in stock. Component engineers use the same Web service to ensure alternative sources of supply and monitor inventory availability.

National Semi has only about a hundred customer accounts to which it sells directly. The bulk of its business is handled through distributors who resell its and its competitors' products. It has private Web sites designed to handle distribution relationships in geographic locations across the world (Europe, Asia, and so on); this capability focused on marketing materials, slide presentations, brochures, product selection guides—everything to help the distributor close a sale.

In 1997, a new capability was added that lets the distributor see into the full value chain. National Semi's channel partners can register customer deals. A customer typically gives the distributor a list of parts it intends to buy over the coming months and the run rates it expects on them. National Semi gives the distributor a commission and profit margin incentive for providing this information, which helps it smooth its own manufacturing and also lets distributors know what's in the order pipeline. Within the first few months, a thousand such deals were registered. Within a year, this had increased to three thousand deals amounting to over $1 billion in forecast leads.

BizQuote allows everyone in the sales and distribution channels to configure a price quote and confirm lead time and availability. Previously, this could be done only by a National Semi branch manager. Now, distributors are in the loop.

Large customers have personalized sites. National Semi account reps choose the information and features they want to highlight and the site is linked to the real-time account status information for that account. The site includes contract information, white papers, and application notes relevant to their business, along with product development status information for customized projects.

Of the estimated 1.5 million design engineers worldwide, 500,000 visit the site monthly. They pull 330,000 product data sheets a month. Whereas 96 percent of all accesses came from the United States or Canada in the early days, 50 percent now come from other countries, including ones where National Semi has no sales presence. It is receiving orders from countries it has never sold in before.

Cultivating Lifetime Relationships

The Internet has always been community-centered, drawing together professionals and academics and generating forums for political groups. Now, Internet businesses are increasingly tapping into the same phenomenon—providing community forums and services for groups they create or discover among potential customers, and building very personalized and customized relationships with individual customers at the same time.

A medium-sized insurance firm in Scotland, formerly called Scottish Provident, illustrates what this new collaboration economy is all about.[6] In 1996, it decided to dump its entire business model, which was the traditional one of providing a mix of products sold through agents, and to focus entirely on a single product set—one that then accounted for just 5 percent of its business. It changed its name to The Life Company and specialized in protection of the individual person. One of its innovations is offering customers a personal health style coach, who is a qualified nurse. David Trafford, a British consultant, pats his now-slim girth and tells how this led him to lose close to thirty pounds in weight. The Life Company pays for periodic medical checkups, which the health style coach reviews with the client. The advice creates shared value. A healthy client is a lower-risk client for The Life Company. One of its relationship offers is to reduce premiums if the client takes the coaching advice. The customer gains and The Life Company gains—and they share the resulting value.

Instead of selling individual products—transactions—the company now focuses on the lifetime relationship. Its cost of selling drops dramatically as a result; the economics of adding a new product to the relationship through this style of shared risk and shared value management also drops—the traditional agency model is hugely expensive and the only real relationship the client has is with the agent, not the insurer. The Life Company uses the Web as its primary sales tool and relationship contact.

The Life Company now has 50 percent of its target market. It's invented a business. This company is not a household name, but it's so typical of what the innovators are up to that you could substitute Amazon, Cisco, Dell, Garden.com, Marshall Industries, or any of the better-known companies that have successfully made the Internet their business base. The message is the same. Think relationships. Collaborate with your customer. Give something away, like the free health checkup, to help build the bond. Change your selling and service structures.

Technology Competitors as Allies

The technology providers that drive the Internet businesses' infrastructures have the same message. Think relationships. Collaborate—especially with each other. Here are comments made in late 1998 by senior executives of three different major Silicon Valley companies:

> "People are kidding themselves if they don't have strong partners."
> "Almost all our business has to be done via partners—we have ten technology platforms to support."
> "Ally or die—it's that simple."[7]

Silicon Valley calls this *co-opetition*—cooperation between suppliers, collaboration with competitors. It's the new equivalent of the description of banking provided in the early 1980s by Walter Wriston, the legendary head of Citibank who made it the world leader in ATMs, credit cards, and cash management: *Cooperate in the morning so that you can compete in the afternoon.*

Ensuring the technology base that guarantees the integrity of business transactions rests on the collaborative capabilities of technology partners. When there's any gap in the integration of the telecommunications, software, hardware, data, and supporting tools, that gap can make tools that work well by themselves totally ineffective. To pick just one example from Hewlett-Packard's own experience: Voice (telephony) and data (computer) communications have for decades evolved via entirely separate technology platforms, providers, regulations, and industries. That has meant that 1-800 number call centers are separate from Internet Web sites as "channels." Now they must converge to offer customers the same unified channel that a Dell or Schwab provides, where the customer can move seamlessly from one to the other. They will converge anyway because the IP protocol and telecommunications *bandwidth*—the basic measure of transmission speed and traffic-carrying capacity—are very close to making phone calls just another form of Internet messages. ("Voice over IP" is here now; the only issue is making it fully reliable and achieving the quality of service for Internet voice that phone companies provide.)

HP is an IP provider via its hardware servers and software, but it's not in the telephone switching equipment business. Nortel is a leader in that area, and it's moving fast into the IP world, which is obviously the future of telecoms. Nortel isn't experienced in database management, transaction processing, video, image, printing, and the other components of data networking. HP lives in that world.

In the Internet world, collaboration must include competitors, too. HP, for example, has aligned with Intel to develop a scalable common hardware platform for UNIX and NT—a new industry-standard architecture for the open systems of the future. HP and Intel cooperate on this, while simultaneously competing at the end-user customer level.

Switch focus and look at this from the point of view of a hypothetical but typical business looking to compete in the .profit phase of the Internet. It's obviously very dependent on its technology providers. (eBay found that out when its network—that is, its entire business—collapsed for twenty-two hours in mid-1999 and the vendor and eBay then spent time working out who was at fault, losing an estimated $5 million in revenue and billions in market value as a result of the crashes.) It wants to unify its business service channels—not Internet *or* call center *or* bricks-and-mortar operations but all of these. But its star computer hardware provider isn't a voice equipment provider, and the reverse. And neither business is a database software leader. Nor a digital cellular phone company. Nor a local area network provider.

The hypothetical company is used to getting the best product at the best price from the best provider. As its integrated telecommunications, computing, and information management platform becomes its IP business base, it will start looking to get the best end-to-end business solution at the best quality of service—and good price—from. . . . From whom? The best alliance providers.

The announcement of an alliance is easier than the implementation, of course. It demands collaborative competence—a culture and not an ad. As industry insiders, we could dish up many juicy stories about the double crosses, cultural clashes, mismatches, and unexpected breaches among allies as their interests diverge or conflict. There's the one where an international telecommunications company was scheduled to make a major announcement of a joint venture with a U.S. megaplayer at noon, only to hear at 10 A.M. over the newswires that the very same "ally" had just joined up with the smaller firm's main competitor. Or the very same megaplayer's chairman leaving the chairman of another megaplayer waiting in the first class lounge at Heathrow for the meeting to finalize a merger agreement, completely unaware that the head of the other firm was at a press conference in the U.S. announcing its acquisition by yet another megaplayer.

The message here is that collaborations and alliances that work are now more important in technology than specific products. In addition, they are core to both technology providers' business models and to their business customers' business models. Choose providers that are good alliance-makers; avoid those that aren't. And be a good alliance-maker, too; don't treat your strategic technology providers as "vendors."

Collaborating with Service Partners

For an online securities trading firm to build a relationship base with its customers, as opposed to just offering transactions—trades for a fee—means offering them a wide range of services and support for those services, much of which is completely outside your own competence and operations. So you build your brand on the Internet less around your product than your relationship resources. E*Trade is an instance of this. For it to build a strong base of repeat customers, it needs many partners. It has marketing relationships with Yahoo, Sprint, and AOL. Market information comes to its Web site customers through TheStreet.com and chart data from Big Charts, a subsidiary of Marketwatch.com.

The complexity of the technology base for large-scale Internet transaction management in itself demands an ever-growing collaboration between the Internet business and its hardware, software, and telecommunications providers. Only that collaboration can guarantee the integrity of the transaction, the center of commerce on which relationships are built. Scalability—being able to add capacity fast to handle ever-increasing volumes and customers—plus security, availability, response time, and reliability all strain the capabilities and products of the providers; that's why they have to collaborate on behalf of the customer.

Building Collaborative Competence with the Management Agenda

No firm can plan its way to .profit unless it has accurate, meaningful, and usable information about what generates profits. That ought to be common sense, but a constant problem throughout the history of information technology has long been a simple but bedeviling reality: infrastructure costs come now and benefits much later. The benefits will also often be impossible to forecast reliably, especially when they rest on such intangibles as better customer service or faster time to market. Infrastructures do not in themselves generate benefits, they enable them. Many of the costs are hidden and not adequately included in the business justification. For instance, every dollar spent on systems development typically generates four dollars for maintenance and operations over a five-year period. A $2,000 purchase of a personal computer is the loss leader for all the networking, data management, service and support, security, and operations costs that are required to make it an effective business tool.[8]

The benefit side has been even more problematic in every way, and many senior executives are deeply skeptical about anything promised in their IT unit's business proposals. When a technology investment displaces costs, then it's possible to calculate the savings. When, though, it creates something new—closer customer relationships, faster distribution, better communication, more effective knowledge management, improved forecasting—forecasts belong more in the domain of science fiction than of business. This is not unique to any infrastructure-based large-scale innovation. Economists and historians have been unable to pin down the payoffs from the Industrial Revolution and from the railroads—it takes time for the payoffs to become clear. Similarly, how do you put a specific figure on the value of your education? For example, what's it "worth" for you to take an evening or weekend program on electronic commerce?

We don't have precise figures and reliable methods for assessing the infrastructure payoff calculus for Internet business. No one does. When you are dealing with rates of market growth of 40 percent a quarter (typical for high-flying Internet growth businesses) or 70 percent a year (the trend line for the Web as a whole over the past four years)—then it's tempting to rely on managerial common sense and experience and base investment decisions on broad measures of market success, such as revenues and customers. That won't work. The stakes are so high now that companies can't just plow ahead and spend money in the hope of eventually becoming profitable. We recommend four priorities for the management agenda:

1. Focus on the economics of relationships: repeat business, customer self-management, incremental margins, benefits of digital scale through a first-rate technology platform, cost displacement and revenue enhancement through collaborations (the benefits) and customer acquisition, pricing trends, and infrastructure investments (the costs).
2. Leverage immediately all the proven value drivers that offer tangible economic payoffs, most obviously in logistics.
3. Understand that the established accounting methods were never designed to handle the world of intangible assets and the Internet. Make sure that when you are reviewing "costs" and "benefits" you focus on capital and cash flow.
4. Above all, view marketing, customer acquisition, and support infrastructures as capital and separate them from variable costs.

Then and only then do you have the information to make .profit rather than .com assessments.

As we've seen, the ability of providers and users to work closely together in a true partner relationship increasingly determines the success of both. The same principle applies to the business user as to the technology industry: you can't go it alone and you are only as strong as your weakest ally. Collaborative competence—trust, openness, keeping promises, and readiness to share information—is the hallmark of the culture for Internet .profit business.

The implementation of a company's business model must build on that collaborative competence in relationships with supply chain partners, with players who create new *ecosystems*—value-generating networks—and with technology and service providers. It will center on how to build and sustain customer relationships and how to define and reach key communities so as to customize the company's offers and help its own customers extend their network of relationships. The watchwords: Collaborate or die. Build relationships or die. Reach communities or die.

Here's our advice to business managers:

- Take a hard-nosed look at your firm's collaborative competence—are you an Olympic gold medalist or an also-ran?
- Inventory your alliances across your service base, your technology partnerships, and your relationships.
- Start thinking about how to make collaboration your source of capital leverage.

The business imperatives discussed in Part Two provide a logical, ordered path to collaborative competence—and .profit.

The Value Imperatives of the Internet Space

4

CRAFT THE BUSINESS MODEL THROUGH THE VALUE IMPERATIVES

Any strategy based just on technology is but a hope.

A firm's .profit business model is a focused differentiation that offers something special and new in the marketplace. By definition, it's unique to the firm. And it's special and new, otherwise it's just an online alternative to an offline customer option. There's no off-the-shelf business model, which means that there are few established guidelines to draw on. Nor can executives easily evaluate the experiences of other companies. Hundreds of business models came out of the race to .com, and new ones are being invented and tailored to the value agenda so fast that the press reports read like Hollywood gossip rather than business analyses. We won't know for many years if any of the business models being tried out will actually succeed, especially those that are centered on entirely new pricing schemes and relationships. So it's here that executives must put their ingenuity, effort, and rigorous thinking.

The business model is the statement of basics, the company's direction along the value path. It defines the end and the technology part of organization, processes, and collaborations make up the main means. In the .com era, it was very much the other way round for many companies;

technology was the end. Companies hoped that a Web presence would ensure they were at least in the competitive game. They relied on the technology to generate the business advantage—and it hasn't worked out that way. There's not a single .profit leader that got there just through having a Web site. What positions firms as gorillas or baby gorillas is the set of business principles they adopt that focus their strategy, that differentiate them from the standard .com players, and that also recognize what makes Internet business a unique new opportunity.

Each of these is critical for success. Focus translates into clarity of priority: markets, customers, relationships, channels, marketing, and organization. Without established examples and benchmarks, executives just can't see a path to the future, only a broad and often foggy panorama. Differentiation is equally critical and becoming more and more difficult to achieve via just a Web site. For any transaction, there are often dozens of .coms, many of them with pages looking much the same. When they have nothing else to distinguish them, they typically compete on price, a self-defeating tactic in the era of GiveItAwayFree.com and ferocious price-cutting. Finally, merely creating an online version of some service or facility is not a business model; it's just a copycat routine that in many instances is less attractive than its offline equivalent.

There are by now plenty of business models for companies to look at. Amazon, Dell, Cisco, National Semiconductor, Federal Express, Ariba, Yahoo, Chemdex, American Airlines, E*Trade, Marshall Industries, Schwab, eBay, *The San Jose Mercury,* Webvan, AutoByTel, Freeserve, VerticalNet, Wingspan, Mercata, Accompany, Buy.com, Priceline.com, Garden.com, Telebanc. . . . The list could go on and on, but the list itself is not very helpful to managers. Your own company is nothing like any of these. It's unique. You're not a bookstore, so forget about Amazon. There's no way your firm is going to turn its pricing upside down the way Priceline has. Forget about trying to be some new style of vertical trading hub. You don't see paying a small fortune to AOL to be on its portal. And anyway, you don't believe some of these companies will be around a few years from now. Their stock prices go into the stratosphere but then come plummeting down, so what does their sales growth or customer base really amount to? How can you tell?

TODAY'S VALUE IMPERATIVES

Our value imperative framework is built on our broad analysis of the business models and experiences of all the companies listed thus far—plus many others we've worked with and plus HP's own experience. And, yes, you are like Amazon in some ways. And Priceline. And Ariba. But your business model must be unique to your firm, so it doesn't make sense to copy theirs.

This paradoxical statement that you're the same but different is easy to explain. Because the six value imperatives reflect the main dynamics of companies and market responses, they provide what we term business model *templates*. You can use them as guidelines for thinking through the issues of where and how you must build the value that gives you a proactive position in the market. Our templates, which are the topics of the next six chapters of *From .com to .profit*, are the general principles behind the business models of the winners to date in the online marketspace. Our message is simple: focus your Internet efforts on a combination of the value imperatives discussed in the chapters of Part Two. Those value imperatives will guide you along the path to .profit.

The imperatives are about business basics; both the upside opportunity and the downside threat grow by the very fact that they *are* basics. Take logistics, for example. The upside is that your company can take out all the waste in all its many supply chain relationships, create a speed advantage, expand the bounds of its enterprise relationships through new interconnections, and simplify or eliminate business processes that create the opposite of convenience. If it gets well ahead of competitors in the basics of logistics, it fractures their business models.

It shouldn't then be a surprise that as companies either reached the limits of the .com battle for eyeballs and hits or simply failed to balance the capital input and value relationship output, the ones that moved ahead focused their efforts more and more on a business basic with high upside opportunity. For instance, you'd expect an existing leader in a competitive arena where distribution and supply chain costs show up as high overhead and heavy inventories to make this an upside priority. That's why in logistics, the winners in Internet business are almost all well-established companies who were already skilled players: Dell, Cisco, National Semiconductor, Hewlett-Packard, and IBM, for instance. This is not an area where you'd expect many start-ups.

But you *would* expect start-ups in areas where logistics practices have been constrained by limitations on interconnectedness and corresponding information and communication flow. That opens up gaps to fill, and value-adding intermediaries are racing to fill as many of them as they can. The start-ups invent new basics for logistics, such as disposing of excess inventories, reducing operating resource costs, or facilitating reverse logistics, a relatively new field within logistics that concerns what to do with returned goods.

The inefficiency and waste that dominates many supply chains explains why we have seen such an explosion in new B-to-B hubs. And such a wide and deep impact. Chemdex,[1] which runs more and more types of electronic market, has partnered with one of the largest HMOs to create a hub that links hospitals and goods providers of everything from bedpans to bandages. A spokesman was very specific about the reason for the move: "The health care industry is an obvious fit for us because of its size and inefficiency."[2]

Here's a warning about the downside of logistics. If your company doesn't have the business model and supporting technology platform to take the opportunity, then it's committing itself to remain at best average when the leaders will be pulling well away from the midpoint. It may be able to afford not to be a leader in many areas of product innovation, market development, and manufacturing technology, because these are high-risk ventures and only a very few firms will succeed. But it certainly cannot afford to fall behind in the very basics of business. And, of course, that's what logistics is all about.

Information technology generally has the effect of widening the gap between the leaders and the average players in an industry as a given area of application becomes part of the fabric of everyday business. This happened in the airlines when American Airlines used its Sabre reservation system to redefine the basics of industry marketing in the early 1980s. In retailing, Wal-Mart's use of its point-of-sale capabilities gave it the same pacesetting lead. The average players were squeezed and American and

Wal-Mart so stretched their lead that they redefined the competitive rules of their industry.

In those days, the term *business model* was not part of everyday business thinking. Perhaps that's because these and comparable examples did not all at once affect the very basics of the entire enterprise in the way that the Internet so often has. Airline computerized reservation systems (CRS) were part of operations and point of sale (POS) an element in store replenishment. American was not initially the leader in CRS; TWA had superior technology and United Airlines a larger share of the travel agent market. But it was American that first spotted the strategic opportunities of CRS in marketing, distribution, pricing, and customer relationships. Similarly, Wal-Mart did not invent point of sale—Sears had tried it out a decade beforehand—but Wal-Mart turned it into the first and still the largest enterprise electronic commerce base.

In their IT-centered innovations, American and Wal-Mart brought what was originally a relatively minor part of operational efficiency right to the center of business effectiveness. In doing so, they changed the rules of competition. It took a decade for the impacts to work their way across the industry. In the mid-1980s, just about every competitive move in the airlines centered on control of a major CRS, with Delta—the leader in the basics of the traditional business—left very much adrift. Kmart (the retailing leader) never caught back up, spending billions on POS but not closing the gap between Wal-Mart and itself.

The same is the case for each of the imperatives. Winners win through redefining the basics of business performance. Losers lose because however skilled they were or still are in the old basics, the rules have been changed on them. It's the business basics that explain successes and failures, not the .com element per se. For instance, in perfecting customer relationships, it's become very clear indeed that offline business processes (inventory management, order fulfillment, internal coordination to respond to exceptions, and so on) are as important as online interaction.

So the dynamics of Internet business are very similar—but the pace is not. There's so little reaction time available for companies that get left behind. That's why the term *Amazoned* has crept into our vocabulary. It's equivalent to being "Americaned" or "Wal-Marted" by a competitor's moving so fast and effectively to change the basics of an industry that the gap immediately widens, with the average firm unable to respond and several of the leaders left at a standstill, as Delta and Kmart were.

It's all about basics. It's all about time. The risk for any company, however skilled in the basics of today, is that the value imperatives of the Internet business space suddenly change the basics. They fracture the firm's business model.

FRACTURED BUSINESS MODELS

If you've ever fractured a rib, you'll remember only too well just how painful this is. You appear to be fine. Friends may wonder what all the fuss is about. You walk around, talk, eat—and think of almost nothing else but the pain. You can't move quickly and you certainly can't exercise. You are, in the literal sense of the term, healthy: no infections, no change in your weight and cholesterol count, and no apparent heart problems. You are just out of commission.

This analogy is a useful one in thinking about business models. It's best illustrated by Amazon.com, Dell Computer, and Charles Schwab on the one side—healthy business model and ribs so far intact—and Compaq, Barnes and Noble, and Merrill Lynch on the other. All three of these latter companies have been outstanding performers for a decade or more. If the problems they now face were the result of incompetence or blunders, then there would be little to learn from their experience. If they were examples of dinosaurs, unable to throw away their old models and leap headfirst into cyberspace, then all we need say is "Sayonara. You're gone." But these companies are superb. That's the point. A competitor changed the rules and turned "superb" into "vulnerable" at the most basic level of their identity, strategy, and operations.

These are just a few of the best-known examples of leaders in an industry getting a hit in the ribs when they were in their best health. .Com caught them by surprise, but they may well come back. That's why it's best to think of them as suffering from fractured business models rather that broken ones and to then ask what other companies can learn from their situation and their efforts to repair themselves. How do companies learn from this and anticipate where they face the same risk with the same potential impact?

There is no pat answer. There are many areas of business where the Internet was expected to pose a major threat to established business models but so far hasn't. Real estate and insurance, for instance, seemed like obvious targets of opportunity. But to date, there have been no real estate equivalents of Amazon and no insurance giant to match Schwab's disruption of its industry.

That's not the point. The main lesson from the examples we have given is what might be called the Best Defense school of business: get your retaliation in first. Waiting to see if, when, and where a new gorilla will stomp into your territory guarantees that you'll have to react instead of being able to take the lead or at the very least join in the game.

Warning Signs and Hotspots

If you can look ahead and see that within the next few years any of the following apply to your firm, you will be fractured or be able to do the fracturing:

• *The 10 percent customer base or margin factor.* What percentage of your customer base can your industry lose for good and still be viable? What percentage of its margins? The answer for most businesses is that a 10 percent loss of customers and 10 percent loss of margin means death. In retailing, if a mall has a permanent drop in traffic of just 7 percent, it will go out of business. Given that online prices average 10–15 percent below their offline equivalents and given that the logistics leaders have a comparable edge, the management message is, Don't wait for this to happen to you, even if the threat is only from companies totaling 1 percent of the market. Do the fracturing yourself for the next 1 percent of the 99 percent.

• *Logistics.* You're in a business with complex supply chain, distribution, and related business processes—inventory management, warehousing, shipping, and so on. There are delays, high administrative costs, and lots of paperwork. Much of your working capital is tied up in inventory and receivables. Returns of ordered goods are high. Distributors play a major role as an intermediary between you and your customers. If any of this applies to you, move fast. You must do so before you are left behind in the Internet logistics management transformation. On the positive side, look for *any* opportunity to take advantage of the logistics revolution. It will pay off very fast.

*   *Moment of value.* What can you do for a customer now, regardless of where the customer is or what time it is? Customer moment of value contrasts with company place of location. Wherever online service either creates a new moment of value or transforms place of location into moment of value, your firm is in for a change. Consider, for instance, the medical field. It's very hard for people to get fast and personalized information from doctors and hospitals about health issues. If you are able to get an appointment, how long can you sit in the doctor's office and ask questions, chat with your family, come back and ask some more? How do you locate the specialist you'd like to talk to? Where? When? On the Net, any time, anywhere—and no waiting. So far, that has not translated into revenues and profits—and that's not the issue. The medical services business is inevitably going to change. Online business innovation has long been basically about service at moment of value: twenty-four-hour ATMs instead of bank hours, 1-800 catalog ordering, and use of credit cards. The Internet so extends the opportunity that the price of business freedom is eternal vigilance—in other words, watch out for an eBay that's turned yard sales into nonstop moments of value for seller and buyer.

*   *Intermediary value.* In essence, a Web address is a relationship interface—a contact point. Where is it likely to be far more effective than an alternative: a phone call, face-to-face contact with a person, or regular mail? The question is about it being "far more" effective than these, not just cheaper or more convenient.

Taking Action

Obviously, just stating our principles for effective business models doesn't help managers caught in any of these dilemmas and hesitations know when and how to take the lead. They are the input into a simple process that really is about deciding to decide—beginning the mobilization of the organization and getting away from drift. We see four main steps to jump-starting the process of building the .profit business model:

1. *Assess the likelihood of the firm's existing model becoming fractured and look for opportunities to fracture others' models.* This health check is vital for any firm, for even outstanding companies have been caught by surprise by intruders.
2. *Study and evaluate the business model templates.* Learn from the patterns among companies that have successfully combined the principles we've derived from the overall Internet landscape. They provide useful guidelines for shaping your own firm's future.
3. *Decide if it's time to announce a discontinuity.* This is an explicit shift away from viewing the Internet as a part of the natural evolution of the business—an evolution that can be accelerated through leadership—versus the sort of decision Schwab and Banc One have made to shift the entire business. Wal-Mart and MBNA, the leader in credit cards, have both explicitly decided that their strategy will be an evolution that builds on their strengths; when they see the time is right to move, they will then move aggressively. Both evolution and discontinuity are valid choices—but they need to be made explicitly, not left to drift.
4. *Begin to mobilize fast via internal and external marketing.* Make the business model real to employees, investors, and customers. Shift their perceptions from business-as-is to business-as-can-be. Convince them through execution that can-be is moving to will-be—and thus merits a Price/Vision valuation premium versus one of Price/Earnings.

Price/Earnings ratios value the company *as it is,* based on known business performance, likely prospects, and industry context. Quarterly earnings are the obvious main metric. When a company doesn't meet its forecasts and springs an earnings surprise on Wall Street, institutional investors take that very seriously. They bound their valuation within the knowns of the business and its industry and will bid the price up and down on that basis. It's a sensible short-term view.

In contrast, Price/Vision values the company *as it can be.* There's been a long-standing myth about the market being short-term focused. If that were so, then Amazon's shares would sell for the same price as wallpaper, or lower. Instead, the market is assessing Amazon and the Internet technology players on the basis of their business models. The clearer and more convincing the model, the firmer that confidence will be. More important, the P/V companies have a massive capital advantage over the average firm since market valuation is not bounded within relatively narrow ranges as it is for P/E ones. Their high valuations enable them to make acquisitions for exchange of shares that are in effect free. They pay out no cash. They also aren't held down on their expansion by the need to produce earnings. Crazy or not, it affects us all.

THE MANAGEMENT AGENDA: ASSESS THE MODEL

For us, leadership is about taking the organization to someplace where it's not on track to go—making a management difference. Every firm—or nearly—will get to .com. Much of what is happening as a result needs no executive intervention. Firms will go with the flow and use the Internet to provide real benefits. But this will merely steepen the growth curve along the current path—more customer retention, more sales, more communication. It will all occur *within* the business model of today. That model may well hold up but it should not be a decision by default to work strategically within the givens of that business model. Stay alert to the changes and it's hard to see that any *existing* business model can be taken as "business as usual." For success, it's business most unusual.

We can't see any option for a firm except to take a fundamental look at the basics of the new business landscape and define the business model to address them. Doing so won't always require major online initiatives but it will include an assessment of the impacts of other online players on the value imperatives. For example, it doesn't matter what area of retailing a company is in; it now has to factor into its planning the 10–15 percent price erosion that Internet business creates. Its business model may remain focused on bricks and mortar with its Web site a secondary channel but it will still need to address channel harmony: for instance, handling returns to a store of items that were originally bought online.

That's why we suggest that companies begin their business model review by focusing on the issue of fracturing. Where is their current model (which may be simply a set of historical practices and long-held assumptions) in danger of being damaged in the basics? Where can they do the fracturing? It's essential to forget about traditional competition. Anyone can be your new competitor, just as anyone can be your partner. Ignore industry labels. And don't get blindsided or attacked from the rear.

Figure 4.1 shows two views of the business landscape: a helicopter view from above and a view from the ground. The savvy business executive is looking ahead, is highly focused, is constantly scanning the landscape, all while keeping the goal in mind. That's today's line of sight. To the sides—in the executive's peripheral vision—are the worlds of technology and of business competition. Given the stress, pace of change, and competitive pressures companies face, it's essential to maintain focus and not get distracted. So the clearer the line of sight, the more effective the executive. When a strong company gets caught by surprise by a new intruder, it's generally not because of incompetence—it's because the intruder has not been in business management's line of sight. With the Internet (and the changes it brings) come more and more attacks from outside the line of sight.

Companies are blindsided by players from outside their sphere of vision, in terms of both competitive strategy and exploitation of new technology. In some instances they are attacked from the rear, which they've left unguarded. The executives are on the ground, there are plenty of walls in front of them, fog around them, and thicker clouds approaching. The walls might be barriers to gathering competitive intelligence, cultural blockages, assumptions, work overload—any of the many forces that lead to loss of vision. No manager can be expected to anticipate everything. We show the unknowns as gorillas hidden in the fog and Yahoomazon low enough that the wall blocks the view. When managers scan the landscape, they focus on what they need to deal with in the near future and their view of information technology is generally limited to its governance—steering committees, business justification, and budgets. They may overlook competitive shifts and customer trends that are in their peripheral vision and vaguely seen. The clouds? If they can't identify them, they may be blind to issues that later turn out to be of fundamental importance for .profit business. An example is the vital importance of integration and architectures: the integration of processes and Web site operations, and the technology architecture for meshing all elements of the firm's telecommunications, information, and software resources. And

Figure 4.1. Management Line of Sight

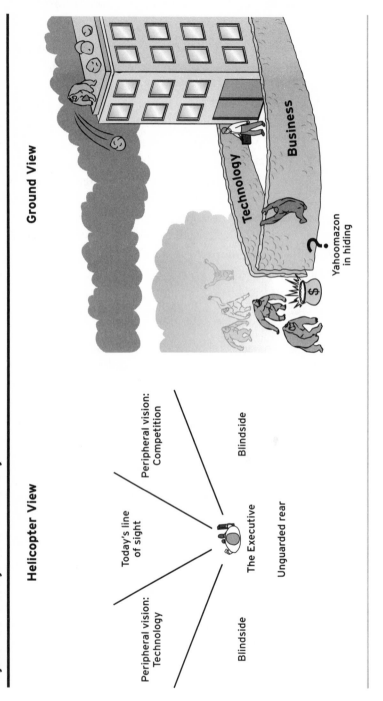

Helicopter View

Peripheral vision: Technology

Today's line of sight

Peripheral vision: Competition

Blindside

The Executive

Unguarded rear

Blindside

Ground View

Technology

Business

Yahoomazon in hiding

hidden out of sight at the rear, the new gorillas are coming, racing at Internet speed.

Executives and managers need higher vantage points from which to assess the landscape, spot the Yahoomazons, and scan 360 degrees. Our book provides a helicopter view, a detailed set of pictures for executives and managers on the ground to use to map the territory and build the .profit business model.

Table 4.1 sets forth a simple checklist to start the process.

You may want to come back to this table after we fly the helicopter for the next six chapters.

Table 4.1. Mapping for the Model

The value imperative	What's in our line of sight now?	What's happening just a little out of our view?	How do we make sure we don't get blindsided or hit from the rear?
Logistics			
Relationships			
Channels			
Capital and cost structures			
Branding			
Value-adding intermediation			

5

PERFECT YOUR LOGISTICS

If you're not a player in the logistics game, you're out of the business game.

L ogistics is too often an organizational orphan, with responsibilities scattered around among procurement, supplier relationships, shipping, invoicing, inventory control, warehousing, accounts payable, accounts receivable, and the like. But companies whose senior managers have adopted and attended to the orphan of logistics—companies that are leaders in integrated supply chain management—dominate their marketspace. They have a cost, time, service, and price advantage that pushes even the best product-based competitor onto the defensive. Consider Cisco: its overhead isn't half that of its competitors by accident. Nor is it by casual luck that Ariba.com has built a loyal following of customers that routinely reduce, by about 20 percent, the costs of the basics—office supplies, stationery, mundane services, furniture—that amount to 30 percent of most companies' costs.[1]

These savings go straight to the bottom line. Use of such business-to-business hubs cuts prices of goods and services typically by 5–15 percent through auctions, disposal of spare inventory, matching of buyers and sellers, and handling of much of the administration that adds up and up and wastes resources and money.[2]

The Internet accelerates every trend and opportunity in logistics, pushing it to become an enterprise-wide strategic priority and no longer a poor orphan. It's demanding—and it can be the best business friend a company could ever have. Take a look at your costs of working capital, lead times for supply chain transactions, costs of supplies, and selling, general, and administration reported on your income statement. Consider what your profit picture and balance sheet could look like if you improve performance by just 20 percent a year. Think of what happens if you don't make that change—and your primary competitors do. Then do it, while time is on your side.

The business goal here is not just to improve your logistics, but to perfect them:

- Make end-to-end logistics your enterprise-wide business priority, taking out waste, steps, delays, and costs everywhere.
- Make your supply chain and related business relationships in themselves a source of mutual competitive advantage.
- Turn logistics from administration to business development, from waste to asset.

The Internet has become a logistics toolkit. Take any element of buying, storing, shipping, paying for, financing, or accounting for *any* type of goods or services, and you'll find a Web hub, software provider, or supply train partnership that offers a step shift—not just an incremental improvement—in cost and efficiency.

THE LOGISTICS ADVANTAGE: SAVINGS

Whereas in many areas of Internet business, most of the talk is about what will happen in the future and what the benefits will be when that promised—or hypothesized—future comes to be, the logistics benefits are there right now and very much non-hypothetical. There's a good reason for this: the Web is a new vehicle for continuing a twenty-year-old journey.

Throughout the history of electronic business, the main driving force has always been business-to-business commerce (B-to-B) rather than business-to-consumer commerce (B-to-C).

B-to-C is the more newsworthy and glamorous. AOL's 20 million customer base, Amazon's almost monthly entry into new markets, Priceline's innovation in letting the buyer state the price, and eToys' 1999 Christmas foray into the retail market all are simple to understand. Plus they all have drama: Will Amazon go broke? Can Barnes and Noble come back? Will eToys kill off Toys "R" Us? There are heroes and villains in these stories and the drama of the ever-dangerous tightrope walk to profitability across a whitewater ravine.

By contrast, most B-to-B Internet business is truly dull. It's mainly about the administrivia of spare parts, office supplies, purchase orders, inventories, invoices, maintenance, accounts receivable, and such. We're unlikely to see a headline in USA Today about the details: "Auto maker cuts purchase order processing cost from $85 to $4!" or "Bank saves 4 cents per pencil!" But there really are headlines there, like "IBM saves $750 million on supply chain management costs" and "HP saves $1.4 billion in inventory costs over three years." These certainly vouch for the logistics payoff. As Bob Wayman, HP's chief financial officer, said in a speech in late 1999:

> We work with 110,000 different suppliers around the world. We maintain the largest parts database in the world. In fact, we have 205,565 different parts numbers across 258 categories of products. . . .
>
> As a result of our many supply chain initiatives, we've been able to compress the chain from monthly to hourly. . . . HP's channel inventory is the lowest in history and HP's inventory-driven costs have declined by more than 20 percent each quarter this year.
>
> Over the past few years, we've been able to decrease inventories as a percentage of revenues from 16.7 percent to 13.8 percent, which translates into savings of $1.4 billion in inventory costs.[3]

HP didn't do this all by itself, of course. One of its allies in logistics is Ariba, the firm that is one of the most successful B-to-B hubs.

Logistics is where the money is—money spent and money to be saved. Logistics is where the time is—time lost and time to be saved. You can add the same for staffing and layers of administration, for reliability, and above all for the ability to match supply with demand.

Think about logistics from different angles:

- In retailing, logistics is about getting the right goods on the right shelf at the right time in the right amounts.
- In banking, it's a matter of providing the right service at the right price at the right time at the right place.
- In manufacturing, it's producing the right goods in the right amounts at the right time and getting them to the right place.

Add to each of these "at the right cost." Logistics is very much a matter of getting things right. Most companies can't, so they rely on expensive hedging of their risk. Inventory is the most obvious hedge. It's a buffer the company can build up (finished goods) or draw on (materials). Accounts receivable are a form of inventory of uncollected funds. So, too, are purchase orders; they are an inventory of goods-in-waiting, items the company needs but that are sitting in the supplier's systems and warehouses. In-transit shipments are another inventory.

This is all waste. All inventory has a carrying cost. It's like the old days of travelers' checks, when the actor Karl Malden glowered into the television screen for American Express, warning: "Don't leave home without them." He didn't mention, of course, that by paying for travelers' checks in advance, you gave AmEx the use of the funds until you cashed the checks. You were paying the opportunity cost of investing the money elsewhere. Companies that carry excess inventory—materials, parts, products, office supplies, receivables, shipments, whatever—similarly have to pay their carrying cost. This is the weighted average cost of capital, which is around 12 percent a year for the average firm. Every million dollars of inventory a firm saves thus adds around 12 percent—$120,000—to its economic value added, its real cash flow rather than paper earnings as shown on the P&L. A firm is effectively borrowing working capital from its shareholders to fund this inventory waste.

In addition to these capital savings, eliminating logistics processing generates even more savings. Consider the logistics of procurement of office supplies. How much paper this involves, how many steps, how much potential for error, how many administrative layers, and how much coordination complexity! In many instances, the cost of the processing is more than the purchase itself. The National Purchasing Association estimates it costs on average $150 to process an order. The online cost is $25–$35.

And this is just the tip of the logistics iceberg. As companies look at the wider opportunity along the supply chain, more and more opportunities emerge to transform costly and cumbersome processes into collaborative interactions along the supply chain and to expand electronic logistics well beyond procurement. Consider the problem for manufacturers of dealing with returns, termed reverse logistics. Estee Lauder, the cosmetics firm, annually sent $60 million of returned goods to waste disposal dumps. It's halved this by using the Internet to provide information about the goods (product codes, bar code data) to retailers and directing them to the most suitable return point. For example, if the problem is that the sell-by date has passed, Estee Lauder has the retailers send the product to a warehouse where the contents are removed—and the containers reused.[4]

Boeing's Solution and Logistics Benefits

Logistics excellence often turns into customer service excellence, too. Boeing, for example, has created a win-win situation in PART, a Web site for its spare parts customers. PART has eliminated 25 percent of Boeing's order processing costs even though it accounts for only 13 percent of orders. It provides savings in personnel, printing, and data entry that in themselves have paid for the site. The main benefits have been intangible and relate to relationships. Boeing's traditional customer contact had been with the purchasing department; now, it has expanded to the real customers—the maintenance engineers and mechanics who use the products.

Time is everything here, for the airline industry works in minutes and hours, not days. The Boeing VP who sponsored PART set as the goal that any customer anywhere in the world be able to get information about its orders in real time. Half of the company's business is high priority. The most urgent is termed *AOG* (for Aircraft On Ground), meaning that a plane cannot take off or be put back into service without the part.

Boeing's spare parts business amounts to $1.2 billion a year and its customers are located everywhere across the globe. They use a world of languages and many do not speak English. There is a 30 percent error rate and corresponding labor-intensive administrative burden to Boeing in handling high-priority orders from these customers. They amount to 20 percent of the total. In addition, another 20 percent of all orders come in by fax, mainly from distributors in places like Africa, who service airlines that have difficulty for reasons of language, size, finances, and politics in establishing direct business relationships with foreign suppliers.

Boeing now offers same-day service for AOG situations, and ships within two hours. For regularly scheduled and lower priority orders, the goal is to be ready to ship by 7 A.M. the next day. Smaller customers (who provide 40 percent of Boeing's spare parts revenues) and customers with AOGs require the same level of service as larger and scheduled ones but cost much more to service.

Boeing has several teams in place to answer customer queries and manually input orders from fax and phone messages. Thirteen people deal with the clerical aspects of the two thousand orders a day that come in outside the electronic data interchange (EDI) system. Seventeen others work three shifts a day to provide inventory, order status, and parts information, handling around three hundred requests a day. Another fifteen handle nine hundred AOG-related phone calls a day. In addition to all this, the Spares Technical Information team deals with such queries as interchangeability of parts, researching and reviewing drawings and standards documents to make sure customers get what they need.

Boeing is as automated as most large companies. It has used EDI for many years. It employs state-of-the-art CAD/CAM. But its interface with the customer was very weak. It had to spend money with no added value to handle non-EDI orders. Staff often spent many minutes dealing with trivial queries for which the answers could have been made available if they were able to access Boeing's databases. Its staff handled twelve hundred phone calls a day, with an abandonment rate—meaning that customers didn't get answers to urgent questions—that its management viewed as "unacceptably" high.

Enter the Web. Boeing launched PART in late 1996. It was a front-end customer interface to a software application originally written in 1973 and rewritten in 1990 to handle spare parts. It provides a direct customer access to the very same systems and databases Boeing's staff have been using for more than a decade. It opens Boeing up to its customers—a move that many business units were initially wary of, especially in terms of security and infrastructure integrity.

The PART system combines an intranet—an internal company site that uses Internet technology—with public Internet access. PART has two main functions: keying in orders and receiving automatic acknowledgment, and accessing information about parts, order and shipment status, and inventory availability. After eighteen months of operation, it was being used regularly by half of Boeing's eight hundred customers. It handles more than four thousand transactions a day. Most of the usage initially was by U.S. customers because many European and other international customers did not have Internet access from their offices. Some European customers took the paperwork home with them to access PART via their own ISPs.

Orders over PART amounted to 13 percent by the end of the first year. Orders via telex-based EDI dropped from 31 percent to 21 percent. The percentage of phone call orders halved. Business grew by around 30 percent because of an expansion in airline traffic worldwide—and Boeing did not have to add staff. It estimates its total order processing costs were cut by 25 percent.

Boeing has also gained revenues. Some replacement parts are proprietary to Boeing but there is a large and competitive market for standard parts, with Boeing's competitors offering lower prices. PART has helped make speed, not price, the premium. The customer can now access Boeing and get information faster than from its competition, place an order, and be sure it will be fulfilled quickly. Customers report many savings. Because they enter the orders directly, they reduce errors and returns and also reduce their own paperwork and labor costs.

Maintenance engineers responsible for getting the plane off the ground did not have a relationship interface with Boeing for most transactions; those went through the purchasing department, with a typical two-day turnaround. PART provides for a direct relationship; many customers have created access to PART through a PC with a Web browser in the hangar.

The tangible savings to Boeing from PART are relatively small to date. The company can quantify reduction of the costs to print order status reports ($300,000) and avoidance of staff increases to handle business growth. The relationship gains may dwarf these.

The Logistics Revolution Supports Collaboration

Boeing's PART program is typical of the logistics revolution—and revolution is the right term here. The most effective uses of information technology to change the basics of competition in an industry have for decades centered on logistics and inventory-related coordination and streamlining. Indeed, it was this that turned IT into EC. Electronic data interchange began the revolution that the Internet extends and speeds up. It's fashionable in Internet circles to view EDI as a relic of old technology and old thinking, but it's still the core of most electronic logistical relationships. Why? It provides a language for commercial collaboration. A few examples:

- The American National Standards Institute (ANSI) X12 EDI transaction set for a purchase order emphasizes precise definitions for "weight," "payment discount," "item number," and other industry-specific terms.
- The United Nations EDIFACT standard similarly lays out exact definitions for shipping, insurance, trading financing, and customs information on a document, enabling it to be created, transmitted, and processed electronically.
- Singapore's rise to the status of second-busiest port in the world (from number ten) rested on EDI.[5]
- The U.S. automobile industry's fight back from near death in its competition with Japan similarly heavily depended on transforming its logistics via EDI and collaborative relationships with its suppliers. Since 1997 the Big Three U.S. companies and two dozen foreign car makers have been building and testing what will be the world's largest *extranet,* ANX—an industry network built on Internet technology and linked to the public Internet. The sponsors believe that just the EDI component of ANX will save $71 per car. This is a business in which saving $1 adds up to huge savings: the $71 means removing well over $1 billion of waste from supply chain processes. In March 2000, they announced that they will create an industrywide Internet supply chain hub for all the competitors to collaborate. The savings could be in the hundreds of billions worldwide.

- Wal-Mart is by far the largest "electronic commerce" company in the world. We put the phrase in quotation marks because EC has become so identified with the Internet that it's easy to overlook other ways of carrying out logistics online. Wal-Mart made its point of sale (POS) systems the base for, first, streamlining replenishment and inventory management and then joint forecasting and scheduling with its suppliers.
- Airline reservation systems and retail point of sale became the base for coordinating key operations in their industries. For example, American Airlines rose to a dominance in its industry that it sustained for over two decades through its Sabre system. This is usually referred to as a CRS—computerized reservation system—but is more appropriately spoken of in the trade as part of "distribution." That term more accurately captures its role in airline logistics: supply chain management (travel agent relationships), inventory management, and yield management (online dynamic pricing and profit management).

It's worth keeping these pre-Internet successes in mind. EDI, POS, and CRS began a process that the Internet extended and accelerated. Logistics was, is, and will be the core of operational efficiency, productivity, and cost management. That's why so much of the recent action in Internet innovation has centered on logistics and B-to-B. Each month, we are seeing more and more B-to-B initiatives to add to those already in place.

LOGISTICS: END-TO-END BENEFITS

The payoff from logistics is massive. Indeed, it may well turn out to be the single most critical factor for individual companies and entire industries. That's because a leader can generate such an edge in every element of everyday operations that it creates a competitive barrier that just can't be breached. The end-to-end logistics platform thus doesn't in itself build an advantage, it puts the others at a disadvantage—in the basics.

A key concept here is "end-to-end." Don't just tackle this a piece at a time—electronic data interchange for ordering, Web links to suppliers, and so on—but take an "extended enterprise" view of all the relationships you have and streamline them through a combination of Web technology, alliances, and business processes. Use your Web presence to provide an ordering point for customers. Link to suppliers' sites for procurement. Narrow down your supplier base to the ones that, like you, are leaders in logistics business model execution. Over time, link your own intranets to extranets and to the Web. Create Application Program Interfaces (APIs) to add services and collaborations, such as connecting your Web site to UPS for coordination of pickup, shipping, and delivery of goods or to manufacturers' sites to access their catalogs and price lists. Select trading partner hubs that provide everyone with valuable information about prices, customers, sales leads, and so on.

HP's Logistics Revolution

Here's an example of end-to-end thinking and what it leads to. Hewlett-Packard has, quite intentionally, undergone a supply chain management evolution. This was initiated back in the mid-1980s when HP began to streamline the complex mass of processes involved in logistics for its personal computers and printers, using electronic data interchange, SAP enterprise resource planning software, and a complex database management system. This handles $15 billion in goods for thirty-two product lines. Extending this core supply chain architecture out to customers via an extranet increases shipment visibility. Instead of the goods being out there somewhere but quite where nobody knows, they can be located at any stage in their journey. HP works only with carriers that have Internet-based shipment-tracking systems.

The many new reports and bits of status information that customers can adapt to their own needs are among the benefits. The system delivers EDI messages at each stage of the outbound logistics process, including advanced shipment notification, shipment confirmation, and other "transaction sets," with direct links to the carriers' tracing and tracking systems. This has dual benefits to customers and HP. One-third of the complaints HP used to get about late deliveries concerned goods that had actually arrived but the customer didn't know it. Customers were able to cut their inventories by 20–50 percent. The accurate, timely, and automatic information allowed HP to save money and improve service by being able to outsource its warehouse operations.

Once HP added inbound logistics to its supply chain management system, the benefits became even more striking. Previously, less than half of HP's orders for PC components arrived on time. The main problem was lack of information, the inability to find out if, for instance, a broker sat on a shipment for days. Attending to the system meant not that blame could be assigned but that questions could be asked early in the process— and the whole process thus speeded up.

UPS provided HP with its Voyager materials-tracking system, which links HP's materials suppliers, freight forwarders, customs brokers, and carriers. This speeds up the processing chain and provides previously unobtainable information about exceptions and alarms. For instance, the freight forwarder is asked to send a message to HP when it receives the shipment and another when it sends the shipment to the carrier. For air shipments, an alarm goes off if HP doesn't receive the second message within twenty-four hours of the first. On-time deliveries have improved from 50 percent to 80 percent, with a substantial drop in inventory levels.

All this is great for HP, but what about for you? HP's considerable experience points to the fact that the only constant in supply chain management is change. Warehouse sites are relocated. Intermediaries may go out of business. Customs procedures will vary across the world. Change happens. Be ready for it.

Payoffs from Logistics

We could pile up page after page of examples of the payoffs from the logistics advantage. Logistics has benefits in the areas of general supply chain management, procurement costs, purchase prices, inventories, errors and delays, shipping and delivery, operating resources, and overhead. In the following sections, we provide a few representative figures and vignettes that need little if any comment—except perhaps one reminder. Perfecting logistics is not a matter of simply a .com. There's a great deal of hard work involved in process design, relationship building, use of electronic data interchange standards, choice of supporting technology, and handling of legal, control, and security issues. It takes attention to detail and the big picture—simultaneously and across the organization.

General Supply Chain Management. Win-win supply chain optimization is a growing feature of online business. A few examples:

- Ryder is a third-party logistics firm, like UPS, that handles all elements between an order and delivery—warehousing, shipping, and customs— with the Internet the coordination link. It estimates that "world class" supply chains have a cost advantage amounting to 3–7 percent of revenues.
- Chipshot.com is able to sell customized golf clubs made at the very same Taiwanese foundries that make Calloway and Taylor Meade products, to the same specifications, at 50–70 percent of their prices. Here, the savings from an online firm versus a traditional distribution chain are dramatic.
- General Electric cut lead times in its receipt of orders from sixty to ten days. As a result, it was able to reduce inventories from seven weeks to two and a half. Its cost per purchase order fell from $52 to $12. GE reports shaving $500–$700 million off its purchasing costs over a three-year period, cutting labor costs by 30 percent, and materials costs by 5–20 percent.
- UPS reports that it cut the supply chain management costs of hospitals using its Web-based distribution services by 40 percent. These constitute 30 percent of their total cost, so that the bottom-line payoff is 10–15 percent.
- For years, Bay Networks, one of the top ten telecommunication equipment companies (and now part of Nortel), tried to get daily information from its distributors so that it could better match production levels to demand. But many of its distributors tracked sales only weekly and would have to change their own ordering software systems to meet Bay's needs. Bay's Web site now enables them to check what routers are available today and what will be available a week from now. They can check shipment status through a link to Federal Express. Bay in turn can see how many orders are being placed and step up production in peak periods. This is the collaboration imperative in action.

"It used to be Company X competing with Company Y," observes Jon Kirkegaard, vice president of logistics operations for i2 Technologies in Irving, Texas. "Now it's supply chains competing with supply chains."[6]

Procurement Costs. It makes more and more sense for companies to use a hub that brings together the buyer and supplier communities in a complex supply chain. In fact, these hubs are now among the fastest-growing segments of Internet business.

General Electric's Trading Partner Network (TPN) is one of the earliest trading hubs. GE built TPN for its own procurement and then turned it into a service for other companies. Its incentive was simple. The "Jaws of Death" were closing fast on GE. Its material costs increased 16 percent between 1982 and 1992, even though the prices were dropping. GE was not getting the best deals through its traditional supplier relationships. Worse, its own prices had been flat and were beginning to decline. Over 25 percent of its 1.2 million invoices per year had to be reworked because of some error or mismatch of information. The amount of paper required to assemble the specifications for a request for quotation on a bid to supply GE was so large that GE often sent the RFQ to only two or three companies.

Once GE launched TPN, all this changed radically. First, it could reach out to a much larger supply base and encourage bids from smaller firms, firms that had been outside GE's traditional supply chain. There's a widely quoted story about GE's Lighting Division needing new machinery urgently and broadcasting a RFQ. Seven new suppliers responded, one of which was a small firm in Hungary, which of course won the bid. This was all done in under two days. The old purchasing system required as many as twenty-two days to develop and distribute the RFQ, and many days to review bids. GE Lighting has reduced its cycle time for machine parts from a week or two to a day and cut staff by 50 percent.

When GE made TPN available to other companies, it quickly became a major hub. Con Edison used the system for electronic handling of RFPs—and cut procurement costs by 30 percent. GE has been able to enhance its minority and small business relationships; TPN reaches out to them via the Internet with software that is downloaded at no charge. TPN makes any firm that uses it more effective by enabling buyers to focus on the strategic components of processes versus the transactional ones.

Purchase Prices. GE also saves 3–5 percent in prices on bids for supplies through TPN. IBM cut its procurement price costs by 9 percent by making the Internet its procurement base, with 65 percent savings in inventory carrying costs. By using Chemdex's trading partner hub, buyers of specialty chemicals pay a 5–10 percent commission to it versus the typical 40 percent markup to brokers and distributors.

Prices of any goods obviously reflect supply and demand but they also are strongly influenced by information availability and suppliers' access to buyers and vice versa. In the Chemdex example, brokers had the information and the access and hence also had the price edge. An in-depth research study of the price paid by winners of bids on two auction sites for business-to-business goods found that they averaged 25 percent less than the catalog prices for the very same goods sold at the very same site. For items where the buyer would need to go to a different site to find a catalog offering, the price difference is even higher—39 percent.[7]

Inventories. As we've said, inventory is waste. It ties up capital and by that very fact dilutes shareholder value. The leaders in logistics remove that waste and also gain flexibility. A 1997 study of best practices in logistics concludes that the leaders have the following advantage over the median performers: 50–80 percent lower inventory and 40–65 percent edge in cash-to-cycle. Their overall costs are 3–6 percent lower as a fraction of revenues.[8] Bear in mind that that figure of 3–6 percent is also the average net profit margin for manufacturing companies.

Dell is the most obvious and striking example of what this advantage amounts to. Its sales in 1993 were $2.6 billion, with inventories $342 million. In 1998, it sold almost five times as much on 50 percent lower inventory levels. Gateway, Dell's nearest equivalent in direct selling, had half Dell's 1998 sales but slightly larger inventories: $6.3 billion in revenues and $249 million in inventory. In 1999, Dell was turning its sales inventory over sixty times a year, versus seven to eight for Compaq. This means that Dell can launch a new product or use new components and get them to the market in around a week. For Compaq, the delay is eighty days. What's the value of Compaq's old products in this context?

One of the most reliable indicators of a firm's logistics capabilities relative to its competition is working capital levels. Finished goods inventory, accounts receivable, materials, and work in process are not really assets, though they appear as such on the balance sheet. They are expensive liabilities and a poll tax the firm pays to smarter competitors.

Errors and Delays. Where you have paper, you have errors. The original document—say, a purchase order—gets handed off to many departments and staff in the long series of workflows that mark most companies' logistical processes. This is obvious, but a few examples underscore the savings:[9]

- The Campbell's Soup sales force used to spend 40 percent of their time handling errors on orders, which amounted to 60 percent of all transactions. Now, since they've moved ordering online, the error rate is under 2 percent.
- Cisco reports that the number of orders with some inaccuracy in them fell from 20 percent to 0.1 percent.
- A grocery industry association report states that online processing of orders reduced the number of supplier invoices in dispute from 30 percent to close to zero.
- Error rates for Texas Instruments fell from one in twenty-five orders to one in ten thousand.

There are savings everywhere in the supply chain.

Shipping and Delivery. The further along the logistics chain the firm extends its relationships, the greater the payoff. So, for instance, the more tightly linked a company's own online logistics systems are to those of its shippers, the faster the response, the less the paperwork, and the simpler the organizational processes.[10]

- In freight alone, Dell saved $30 million in 1997.
- National Semiconductor's orders go directly to FedEx. Except for receiving an execution record back from FedEx, National Semi is then done with everything. The result has been a reduction in the average customer delivery cycle from four weeks to seven days globally and a cut in distribution costs from 2.9 percent of sales to 1.2 percent.

Shipping is expensive. It amounts to around 11 percent of sales for an online retailer. It's now the largest single cost element in a car—around 15 percent of the sales price. It's complex and cumbersome. It can be a coordination nightmare. So why not let experts handle it? That's the logic and the magic of management by interface. UPS, Ryder, and FedEx are the experts in every aspect of "third party" logistics. Through an application program interface, a firm can quickly have a best practice capability that it could never build for itself.

Operating Resources. As we mentioned earlier, most aspects of logistics are pretty dull, so they don't generate the headlines that online consumer business generates. But that's where the money is. Ariba reports that operating resources—supplies like stationery, furniture, office consumables, travel, routine contracting of services, and the like—make up 30 percent of a typical company's costs. *Every dollar of savings on these goes directly to the bottom line* because operating resources are not part of cost of goods but of overhead. Chevron made $15 million in savings and Bristol Myers Squibb $20 million on simple "front-ending" of the business rules for procurement on their Ariba-based intranet sites. This is one of the major high-payoff innovations in logistics. Ariba provides the tools to create in effect an entire operating resource management department in the software front-end.

The Canadian Imperial Bank of Commerce (CIBC) illustrates the scale of opportunity. CIBC had revenues of $8.5 billion in 1998. It spent $1.2 billion on office supplies and services for its headquarters offices and fourteen hundred retail branches. Each department had its own business rules and processes for handling supplies and services. By embedding those rules in Ariba's customized Web front-end and setting up catalogs for its approved suppliers, it's saved $33 million so far and expects to save 10–15 percent of the total. It encountered some resistance from employees who'd built relationships with local suppliers and didn't want to lose them, but this resistance waned rapidly through education. The $4.99 price that the store down the street offers for a box of pencils looks good compared with $5.52 from the online catalog—until you add in the $30 for offline order processing.

THE MANAGEMENT AGENDA: LOGISTICS AS CUTTING EDGE

Consider how small the operating margins of most businesses are. In the car industry, 5 percent makes a very good year. Supermarkets have to get by on 1–2 percent. Bookstores are lucky to net 3–5 percent. The profit margins on personal computers are now so thin that if a machine sits on the retailer's shelf for three weeks, the carrying cost wipes out the profit. A reliable rule of thumb is that margins in manufacturing will be in the 5 percent range, for financial services 10–12 percent, and retailing 3–12 percent. *Motley Fool* reports that distributors' average net margin is 3 percent.[11]

Online logistics offers the chance to add, say, 3–6 percent to these, and in some cases much more. That is, the logistics leaders have the chance to double their net operating profits. The advantage logistics affords is very real. Dell's overhead as a percent of sales is around half of its average competitor. Is it any wonder that Dell, a logistics leader, is also a .profit leader?

There are, as any manager knows, lots of areas to manage in logistics. With attention to the following points, you will see your logistics improve.

- *Decrease waste* (from standard inventory through process design)
- *Minimize errors and delays* (technology is a big plus here)
- *Control costs* (look at procurement costs and purchase prices, for example)
- *Evaluate your supply chain* (including shipping and delivery) and your business relationship chain

Make a small savings here and win a little bit there and soon the benefits and savings add up. Consider some of the figures cited in this chapter, strung together as a profile of what your own firm might achieve sometime soon as a .profit success:

- Get a cost advantage amounting to 3–7 percent of revenues
- Reduce inventories from 7 to 2.5 weeks
- Cut purchase order cost from $52 to $12
- Improve procurement costs by 30 percent
- Negotiate a 3–5 percent saving in prices on supplies
- Maintain lower inventory levels—50–80 percent lower
- Decrease the number of orders with some inaccuracy in them from 20 percent to 0.1 percent

With changes such as these, your costs are bound to be lower, significantly lower as a fraction of revenues. That is, quite literally, hard to beat.

The Internet's ability to expand the range of logistics relationships to any player in the supply chain is one of its most far-reaching contributions to logistics. It builds communities of collaboration that would be impossible otherwise. It reduces a company's operating expenses and provides a competitive advantage in gaining new customers.

6

CULTIVATE YOUR LONG-TERM CUSTOMER RELATIONSHIPS

Transaction + Technology = The .com trap

Transaction + Technology + Matching price competition = Death by .com

Relationship + Repeat business = Starting the value path to .profit

In the online economy, relationship is all. Transactions are almost literally nothing. The transaction player has to pay out more to get the customer than what its average sale makes for it. It has to match the 10–15 percent price cuts that are typical on the Internet and also faces more and more companies that give its own product or service away free to get the relationship. It loses money on every deal. The relationship player also has to spend money to attract customers. But it recovers that investment by building repeat business, adding new products and services through acquisition and alliances, and collecting referral fees. Once it's well established, it earns still more per customer relationship as a portal that can charge rent for other companies to open onto its electronic parking lot. The relationship leader deepens the customer link through personalization, customization, dynamic interaction, collaboration, and building community.

Talking about relationships is easy. Building and sustaining them is not, either in the offline or the online world. Technology people can build the site and integrate it with the firm's transaction processing systems and information resources. Business people have to turn that design into relationships. Trying to go the other way—design the technology and wait for the relationship—is the .com trap. There's no way it will generate .profit. Instead, it may generate a lot of value to customers who found your low price through a search engine and love your special $50 freebie deal. They'll happily take the price and the deal. Perhaps they'll come back— but if their next search engine result doesn't list your site as the best transaction offer, they probably won't.

There are plenty of .profit lessons to be learned from the fact that 70 percent of Amazon's customers are coming back time after time and that Charles Schwab is able to charge two to three times the commission fee that other online firms charge, for the very same transaction. It's the relationship that earns Schwab the premium.

Thus, one of the most basic principles of .profit is: think relationship. Relationship is critical to Internet business. The following points are fundamental to management understanding and action:

- The cost of acquiring customers is so high that you must find ways of keeping them.
- Relationships exist at the discretion of the customer, not the enterprise. The company must *sustain* its value to customers—in ways that extend well beyond price alone.

Given these basics, the business goal here is

Prepare for the rise of the relationship economy and the death of the transaction economy. Make the Web-customer interface the base for an ever-extending and deepening relationship that becomes more and more personalized, customized, collaborative, and community-centered. In doing so, transform your own revenue and cost structures.

There's a very clear pattern in what the exemplars in perfecting customer relationships do:

Differentiate the offer. Differentiating the offer is tough in itself and becoming increasingly tougher. Besides having a site that is easy to navigate, fast, and reliable, the exemplars often have some special twist beyond the straight sale to get across the message that theirs is not just an online version of a standard sale.

Generate high repeat business. Building repeat business fast is the only way to swim ahead of the financial tide. The catch here is the saturation effect and how quickly it comes in. How many books, airplane tickets, or personal computers will a customer buy? You can't keep selling repeat customers more and more of the same product; you must broaden your business base. The exemplars do this by providing comparison shopping, encouraging self-management, and continuing to personalize and customize.

Build collaboration and community everywhere. The exemplars continue to strengthen the bond with the customer: the companies bring more and more partners to the table and the customers bring more and more community focus. Thus each customer becomes part of an extended relationship base. Community is the binding force of just about every aspect of the Internet—its social, educational, political, and business innovations.

Stated bluntly, any company that doesn't build its Internet strategy around relationships rather than transactions just won't make it. Companies must differentiate, generate repeat business, and build collaboration and community. This is what "marketing" is really about. It's also what human resource management is about, because obviously a major organizational transformation is needed to build a culture, skill base, and reward system that can execute all this.

DIFFERENTIATE YOUR OFFER

In the early days of Internet business, the main differentiation was price. The myth was that price was all that customers really cared about. But over time, the Net has become like the airline business: when one player cuts prices, the others have to follow. Customers can easily set their search engine to find the best deal. By announcing your price to your customer, you are also announcing it to your competition. In addition, more and more sites act as intermediaries and locate the best price for customers— sometimes even helping create it. Electronic shopping agents—*bots*—and software brokers are rapidly emerging as the new generation of e-services.

The Internet also eliminates the edge that a number of industries have used for decades in controlling prices: the information gap between buyer and seller. Even ten years ago, it was very hard for someone to find out, say, the best price on a car with specific features, the best deal on a flight, or the best variable life insurance coverage. The auto dealer, travel agent, and insurance agent had better information than the customer. In business-to-business dealing, brokers and distributors similarly could base their fees and commissions on the information gap between providers and customers.

Now that buyers can get wholesale prices over the Internet, many dealers are realizing that they no longer have an information advantage that they can use for bargaining. According to *Business Week,* more than 40 percent of car buyers come into the dealership armed with a printout from the Internet. The CEO of a chain of dealerships told *Business Week* that he's moved to no-haggle prices: "I think the customer will be within $100 of knowing what the price is going to be, so I might as well set it there."[1] Now that consumers have instant access to fare prices from just about every airline, they will no longer accept the vagaries of the industry's complex pricing schemes. And if you want to buy insurance just on price, there are plenty of Web sites that will search out a far better deal than you could come up with by yourself. Car dealers, travel agents, and insurance agents won't necessarily go out of business but they can't compete on just price. Nor can distributors exploit the old information edge, because there's sure to be a hub being set up to bring buyer and seller together—if there's not one out there already.

How, then, do you create a differentiator when price is not it? Obviously, if you have a unique product or service, that in itself will be enough, but that's a rare circumstance. The most successful items in the mass market and everyday business-to-business commerce will, by definition, be ones with high demand and thus likely high supply. No one is going to concede a monopoly position to you. Instead, they are going to imitate your .com—and drive the price down.

One approach to differentiation is to give something away free. That's changing the very nature of business. Another is to price right—instead of setting a fixed price. A third is to follow up the transaction.

GiveItAwayFree.com

CompuBank, which claims to be the first national Internet bank chartered by the federal government and approved by the FDIC, offers free bill payments and free ATM services. Indeed, just about all its services are free of account fees. As an executive stated, "We found we could offer free services because of low Internet overhead costs."[2]

The phrase, "because of low Internet overhead costs," is a key one for businesses both on and off the Internet. It points to a continuation of the trend that has seen electronic mail, Internet site design and hosting, transaction charges, personal computers, and software move toward being free, with phone calls soon to follow. In each of these instances, the giveaway is targeted to building the repeat business right from the start. For instance, by giving away a free MyXYZ site (Amazon, Schwab, Dell, and the rest), a company creates a strong reason for you to become a customer and to keep coming back. This turns the transaction into an opportunity.

GiveItAwayFree is profoundly destabilizing: it can fracture your business model without notice—even if the giver goes out of business. That happened to FreePC, one of the first companies to give a personal computer away free. It was acquired by Emachines, a company that sells low-cost computers, and which made one of the conditions for the deal that FreePC stop its giveaways. Even so, it has still changed the rules of the PC retailing business.

In November 1999, American Express announced a GiveItAwayFree play that directly attacks the business model of Internet firms in the same way that Internet firms first attacked those of "old" companies like AmEx. Firms like E*Trade, Discovery, and Ameritrade had launched a .com attack on the securities establishment by slashing trading fees from anywhere between $50 and $100 for a typical transaction to between $6 and $12. AmEx now offers free trades for any customer who maintains a $25,000 account balance—a balance that is very small for AmEx's target market. This is a relationship—long-term account—move, not a transaction play.

This is yet another example of why the death of the transaction economy is inevitable. Any transaction that can be provided online at a low marginal cost will be given away, perhaps not now but within a few years. When that transaction is a company's breadwinner, there is yet more pressure to focus on the relationship—and perhaps give away someone else's product for free.

Use Right Pricing

One of the opportunities that information technology has long provided for airlines is to choose the price to offer to the very next customer. Called yield management, this is the process by which a carrier constantly monitors sales of seats on a given flight and adjusts the price so as to maximize not revenues but profit margins. The goal is to avoid either being left with unsold seats or selling too many at a discount and losing late bookings, for which the traveler would be willing to pay full fare. This system is why the person sitting next to you may have paid a third of what you did.

Yield management adjusts prices to inventory. It's vital to the economics of a business where the difference between a profitable and disastrous year is as little as five additional seats filled per flight. But it creates many anomalies. Business passengers, who are generally more timetable-constrained that leisure travelers and often unable to book a long time ahead, pay more far more for their tickets, even if they provide the airline with plenty of business. The distortions—the "vagaries"—in prices at best puzzle the ordinary person and are harder and harder to explain and justify. Yield management illustrates a broader point: IT can be used to price in real time.

The Internet will always be a laboratory, testing innovations that range from wild idea to tomorrow's IPO, and we're seeing price experiments everywhere. The idea of a fixed price across an industry, with some degree of discount somewhere, is basically over. Priceline.com has attracted attention through its patented pricing scheme by which you name your own price for airline tickets and hotels, specifying the dates you wish to travel. Having met with success with its scheme, Priceline.com has extended into other types of offer, including groceries and even new cars.

The Internet lab is constantly creating ingenious pricing schemes. Accompany.com is one of the firms that exploits group buying power. It negotiates with a supplier to sell a product on a sliding price scale—the more buyers who sign up, the lower the cost for each of them. Others use the processing power of IT and the reach of the Net to handle many types of auction—English, Dutch, and Yankee. Still others sell below their own cost, looking to make up the loss through fees from advertisers and sponsors.

It's not yet clear which of the pricing lab experiments will be successful. General Electric tried auctions on its TPN (business-to-business hub); they bombed, even though the site has been one of the biggest successes in Internet business. eBay has made auctions an addiction for millions (and in the process driven down the prices of Beanie Babies). There are discount schemes everywhere, rewards for frequent buyers, personal deals targeted to a consumer on the basis of information about previous purchases, interests, and shopping behavior.

Regardless of the outcomes of these and other innovations, fixed pricing is close to over. To differentiate the transaction, you need to differentiate the pricing. This will certainly be a major element of e-services as the .profit era moves forward. That's because the standard .com transaction storefront, which offers the same price to everyone with discounts for some, is moving to a market complex in which prices are brokered, offers assembled, bids made, and deals personalized. Price is not the differentiator. Pricing is.

Follow-Up

A third approach to differentiating the transaction is to follow it up. That starts with careful segmentation. You are looking not just for customers but for customers with whom to build a long-term relationship. Early Web e-commerce sites aimed at getting the broadest reach into a mass market. The issue was getting surfers to your site and turning them into buyers. .Profit approaches target customers and markets much more selectively. NextCard, for instance, sells credit cards only over the Net. It places 12 million online ads a day on other sites and gets a tiny response rate—just 0.4 percent. But that translates to $30 million in new account balances a month, with customers maintaining balances of twice the industry average of $2,700. Charge-off rates are half the typical—and costly—average of 5.5 percent for Visa accounts. NextCard has cut its customer acquisition costs by 70 percent in a year. The key is which sites it chooses to place its ads on. It's creating a new style of segmentation via online demographics.

If you have attracted the right customer, then the *first* purchase is the relationship opportunity. That point should be obvious, but the .com transaction mentality still seems to dominate business practices on the Internet. In late 1999, Rubric Inc. surveyed fifty people, each of whom made a $50 purchase on one of fifty top Web sites. The questions were directed toward determining whether the company treated them as valued customers it wants to do more business with. The results are summarized in Table 6.1. You may have an Internet strategy even if your customers would give mostly "no" answers to these questions—but you don't have a relationship perfection business model. Your company will live or die by the transaction.

GENERATE HIGH REPEAT BUSINESS

The incremental margins on online repeat business are generally very high. That's mostly because the expensive cost of acquiring the customer gets rapidly amortized and the company starts to gain the benefits of non-bricks and mortar operations. So, for instance, Amazon's auctions and CD sales attract its already loyal book buyers. Amazon has an astonishing 70 percent repeat business rate with its auction margins in the 80 percent range. That's also why eBay became profitable so fast; its operating margin is 70–85 percent depending on the season. B-to-B hubs similarly have

Table 6.1. Does the Company Really Care?

Query	Percentage Responding "No"
Did the site ask you if you wanted information on related products?	57
Did the site send a follow-up marketing offer?	84
Were marketing communications personalized?	96
Did the site recognize you as a repeat buyer?	75
Did the site respond to your e-mailed questions?	40

high incremental margins and lower customer acquisition costs than B-to-C firms. Chemdex has averaged a 50 percent margin, for instance.

The ideal product to sell online is one that is expensive to buy and cheap to ship. Books, CDs, and airplane tickets fit that profile well. But as a senior executive from Wal-Mart commented to us in late 1999, the Internet winners all "plucked low-hanging fruit." It's somewhat tougher to make money out of selling, say, toilet paper over the Web. The main problem is illustrated in *Forbes* magazine's analysis of the economics of a retail superstore versus an online store, shown in Figure 6.1.

There are several obvious points to make about the figures presented in Figure 6.1, which are representative of the fundamental cost dynamics of most Internet business, even though the specifics will vary across types of business. First, the online retailer has the big advantage of no sales tax. This offsets most of the shipping and handling burden. But the big difference is the 17 percent for marketing. If the online player can

Figure 6.1. Relative Costs of a Retail Superstore Versus an Online Retailer

	Superstore	Online
Average sale	100	100
Discount	(10)	(20)
Shipping and handling	0	11
Sales tax	7	0
Customer pays	97	91
Cost of sales	(67)	(58)
Cost of service	(3)	(10)
Gross profit	27	24
Rent	(1)	(5)
Labor and store expenses	(11)	(0)
Web site	(0)	(3)
Marketing	(3)	(17)
Net profit	12	(1)

Note: Parentheses indicate negative values.
Source: Data from *Forbes,* March 1999.

cut this and cut the shipping and handling premium, it will make a lot of money. Otherwise, it won't. Get the marketing cost down to 3 percent and the shipping and handling to, say, 7 percent and this is a margin swing of 18 percent. Then, the company makes 50 percent more than the super-store, with a net price edge of about 7 percent (but watch out for sales tax legislation).

So repeat business is simply essential. But it needs to be both repeat business and bigger business. Shipping and handling are largely, though not entirely, the same for a small order as a medium order and a big order doesn't increase them much. A flood of small orders can be too expensive to benefit from, as banks found with ATMs, back when they used to offer free use of the ATM to check account balances.[3]

In late 1999, an industry analyst observed that while Amazon's rate of repeat business continued to grow and had reached 70 percent, its average sale per customer transaction was dropping.[4] That triggered alarm bells among many investors. Time will tell if this is a serious problem but it's certainly a symptom to keep checking up on. Similarly, Ameritrade's acknowledgment around the same period that its customer acquisition cost had increased to $400 (from $200–$250) rang just as many alarm bells, with the same impact on stock price.[5] If .com was largely about getting customers, .profit is very much about keeping them.

Keeping customers requires every skill in the Internet business and technology game—that is, in the relationship game. From the business perspective, the main weapons are process-centered: order fulfillment, error- and exception-handling, response to customer e-mail, ensuring advertised goods are available in inventory, responsible use of customer data and respect for privacy. Further, a return visitor should be recognized and treated as such, and the site must be easy to navigate.

Most sites—especially those of companies with a long history of online business—aren't easily navigated. Prior to the explosion of .com companies and of customers responding to them, electronic commerce rested on specialized online transactions. Electronic data interchange—the substitution of computer-to-computer processing of purchase orders, invoices, shipping instructions, and related documents—was generating huge benefits for many firms, even before the Internet provided a universal, low-cost, and easy-to-access business infrastructure. Automated teller machines, credit card authorizations, and travel agents' use of airline computerized reservation systems are everyday examples of pre-Internet electronic commerce that is increasingly moving from special-purpose, proprietary networks to the Net. The transaction was the unit of commerce: a procurement order, credit card purchase, or cash withdrawal. Each was independent of others; "service" meant convenience and there was limited relationship building.

Consider ATMs. These are transaction factories that perform superbly. They have to; add just one millisecond—a thousandth of a second—to each transaction and, according to Bank of America, you'd be waiting in line literally forever to get your cash, as the electronic traffic jam built up. But transaction factories are not relationship-centered.

This may be why banks—once expected to be leaders in e-commerce—have been laggards. As of mid-1996, their total online customer base was about 500,000, with 350,000 of this total accounted for by Wells Fargo. By late 1999, Wells Fargo had reached a million in customer base but no other bank was anywhere close to this. Compare the customer growth in online securities investment, consumer portals, and airline booking sites, and it's clear that the electronic services leaders of the 1980s are Internet business laggards.

This seems to reflect the transaction heritage of banking technology and staff. The old service sites are in general highly structured and very procedural. They're programmers' sites. All too often, you have to repeat the same steps, enter the same data, respond to a wearying series of questions, and can't easily get back out of the inquisition. A Web site obviously must manage transactions well. Indeed, the key technology agenda is how to guarantee the end-to-end integrity of the transaction—when the transaction doesn't work, forget the relationship. That said, however, the relationship is the business, not the transaction.

And repeat business is its foundation. The Web site and all the processes behind it have to be focused on this. Check out your own company's sites to see how well they work. How do they compare to your competitors' sites? It's good practice to make the comparison, and to make it easy for your customers to do the same.

Provide Comparison Shopping

Make sure your company's Web presence is not just an island, isolated and protected from alien competitors. Invite them in. If you think of a purely transaction site as like a 7-11 store, then it's a place you go to pick up something you need. But when you go to, say, Nordstrom or Home Depot, you typically want to look around and compare products and prices. One reason you choose them is their range of offers.

The same is rapidly becoming the case for the Web sites that customers choose to go back to. United Airlines lists its competitors' fares and schedules. Fidelity even sells its competitors' mutual funds. Fruit of the Loom gives its distributors free Web sites—and allows them to list competitors' products. Schwab's OneSource provides comparison shopping among 620 different mutual funds from seventy providers. The brand is Schwab's.

Unless you open up your company site to provide competitors' information, you're inviting a hub to intermediate. You want to get customers coming back to you, not just coming to you to buy. Otherwise, they will bypass you and use a value-adding information intermediary for prepurchase research. The search for information may well include visiting a specific manufacturer's site to look only at its products, but more generally, consumers rely on a neutral information hub that includes all candidate options and may also locate the best price for an item by searching the Web.

Some e-service offerings are so simple and beneficial that no one is likely to turn them down. Brandwise launched a service in September 1999 for buyers of large home appliances to choose the products that best meet their needs. Potential buyers describe the functions and features that matter to them and Brandwise comes back with information on which merchants can supply them, when, and at what price. As the *Financial Times* comments, "For retailers—whether or not they are online—Brandwise will become a new distribution channel."[6]

This type of intermediation can easily bypass manufacturers *whether or not they are online*—and if they are online that can be a very big problem in that the intermediary may undo the manufacturer's own marketing efforts. So it makes sense to use judo, not boxing. Go with the flow: provide competitors' information and even sell their products. Do whatever makes sense from the perspective of the relationship imperative.

Encourage Self-Management

Comparison shopping is one step toward self-management, a critical step along the value path to .profit. A key principle for Internet business is *turn your back office, overhead, and administrative expenses—liabilities—into the customer's valued front office—assets.*

Once you have a loyal customer, you can begin a process that in many ways is as radical in its economic implications as mass production was a century ago. In both instances, producer and consumer gain, and gain hugely. With self-management on the Internet, the company shifts many of its back office administrative processes to the customer side of the relationship interface—the Web site—cuts its overhead, and saves large amounts of money on handling routine queries. Customers get *better* service in return—more choice, the opportunity to configure their own deals and manage their own accounts, and the famous 24 × 7 availability. With self-management, the company can afford to be online twenty-four hours a day, seven days a week.

Self-management is pivotal in sustaining customer relationships. It transforms cost and margin structures, which is to the provider's benefit, but this comes only if the self-management is to the customer's benefit. Otherwise, it's just bureaucracy and lack of service. That's why the company must first build the differentiation and repeat business base.

Say you heard about a restaurant where you don't get any waiter service. You take a plate and serve your own food—and don't ask for anything special, just choose from what's on the table. If you want dessert, stand up and get it yourself. That doesn't sound attractive until it's called brunch or a salad bar. Then you are happy to do the restaurant's work for it. Self-management in online relationships has much of the same flavor. Yes, you do the work for the company. Yes, you're happy to do so. But you choose to do it—it's not forced on you and if you don't see the value and service, well, there are plenty of other online equivalents nearby. Click.

The economic drivers toward self-management are massive. They largely relate to the part of the income statement called *SGA*—selling, general, and administrative costs—or overhead. A better name might be *waste*—waste of people, time, money, facilities, supervisors, phone lines, and paper. There are so many aspects of everyday business that fall into this category, where customers can do a better job by themselves. For example, Wells Fargo gets 60 million phone calls a year, 80 percent of which are inquiries about account balances. Over half of all calls to an airline reservation phone number don't result in a sale. Each of these is waste—$10–$20 per phone transaction. If—but only if—customers actively enjoy using your Web site as an everyday resource, these calls disappear, replaced by customer-driven transactions at a cost of 1–10 cents apiece.

Federal Express handles around 100 million transactions a day, many of which are inquiries about the status of a shipment. Now nearly 70 percent of FedEx's transactions are Web-initiated and tracked through customer self-management (about 60 million a day). At 10 cents versus $10 a call, this is a huge payoff for FedEx. And it's better customer service. Many companies link their Web sites to FedEx and UPS so that the customer can track shipment status of a purchase instead of having to phone the company, which would in turn have to contact the carrier.

More positively, there are many aspects of everyday operations where it's too expensive to provide the service you'd like, but where the customer can sit down and go through the steps and either do a better job or at least find the online interaction preferable to the alternatives—phone calls, mail, or going to a physical location. That's not always the case, of course, but it's nice to have the option. If you're looking to buy a computer, you'd like to take time to configure it and be able to look at catalogs, try out pricing options, and so on. Then you may like to pick up the phone and talk to a human being to make the purchase.

Similarly, you may prefer handling your own investment account details, rather than calling a broker or 1-800 number. You'd like to be kept informed of transactions, be able to send e-mail, and be sure you'll get a reply. You would also like to get reports occasionally. You do not want to have to provide the same information each time you make a trade. It should all be on file. Above all, you want to be able to do all this when you want, where you want, and in the way you want.

Almost by definition, individuals and company staff who value self-management move more and more of their business to their preferred relationship provider. MCI customers who manage their own accounts online are "the highest value customers we have," with 50–75 percent greater spending than others, longer retention, and lower carrying costs.[7] They are also less expensive to serve. A Dell survey in June 1999 of nineteen thousand of its customers found that there were 75 percent fewer order status calls and 25 percent fewer calls for technical support, but that customer contact was up by a factor of five.[8]

Personalize and Customize: Increase Your Stickiness

Self-management opens up many opportunities to extend the relationship by making it more and more personalized and customized. Personalization is very expensive, however. It may not offer the same natural win-win payoff for customer and provider that you get with basic self-management, where the company saves money and the customer feels in command. Forrester Research estimates that it costs a firm $5.5 million to personalize a site. Most of the expense is to integrate marketing processes with customer data.[9]

Consider the problems of moving a traditional bank online—the initial steps might be largely technical, a matter of getting the basic banking transactions done reliably and quickly. But moving from a bare-bones online bank to a personal, direct banking experience demands a change of personality or culture from the queue-expediting ("Next please!") to the conversational ("Off to your lake home, Mr. Jones?") to viewing conversation as a means of gathering context and context as a means of providing service ("Perhaps you'll need some boating insurance for your trip."). This type of responsive interaction doesn't come cheap, but the expense is well worth it—and it's essential if you want to be an e-services player rather than a transaction one.

For example, Toshiba has found that the introduction of the personal element improves traffic on the site by as much as 25 percent.[10] Dell has achieved similar results in the corporate market for personal computers, growing its market share from 8 percent to 31 percent in two years, by offering "Premier Pages" to corporate customers.[11] These are company-specific sites within the Dell site—sites that incorporate the customer companies' own business rules about authority to order, payment, configuration, and so on, so that customers' management can be sure that employee purchase decisions follow company policy. And Ariba's success is based on the flexibility of its ORMS software, which in effect puts a customer's entire procurement department processes in the Web page. In January 2000 Ariba improved its gross margins to 85 percent and had been cash flow positive for eight successive quarters.[12]

As we saw earlier in the chapter, many of the leaders in .profit online business have adopted the GiveItAwayFree.com approach as the enticement in offering personal and customized sites to consumers and businesses. Their aim? *Stickiness*—one of the 1999 Internet business neologisms. Stickiness depends on working out which services and interactions will get customers to register with your site and keep coming back again and again.

Yahoo started out at the opposite end of stickiness: it was merely a search engine you could use to get yourself from Yahoo to someplace more interesting and useful. Now it has close to 100 million people signed up. How did it do it? Consider just a few of its steps to "sticky nirvana."

- *Personalization.* Everything Yahoo does is aimed at making the site personal for its users—who even get electronic birthday cards from Yahoo, along with a $50-off offer at the online store they use most.
- *Free e-mail.* Users provide basic demographic information in return for the privilege—information that is worth far more to Yahoo than the typical price of e-mail services.
- A *personal home page.* Each user can set up a page to provide quotes on user-selected stocks, local weather forecasts, and news alerts.
- A *ready-made community.* My Yahoo offers direct links to Geocities—4 million personal Web sites, "virtual clubs" that allow people with shared interests to schedule conversations, share content, and post links to other sites. (Yahoo paid $4.6 billion to acquire Geocities, which illustrates both the .profit potential and the cost of offering personal interaction on the Web.)[13]

BUILD COLLABORATION AND COMMUNITY

With personalization and customization comes collaboration and community. The more the company extends the relationship from transaction to real interaction, the stronger the bond. The more that interaction extends across the community, rather than just between individuals, again the stronger the bond grows. Rather than keep repeating the words collaboration and community, and with apologies for adding another funny-looking word to the e-everything vocabulary, we'll call this *co-relating*—joint, interactive, dynamic, beyond the individual *and* beyond the company itself. There are other "co-" words that have been coined to capture various elements of all this: co-opetition—collaboration among competitors—and co-creation, for instance. These join the old vocabulary, which has lost its hyphens from long use: cooperation, coordination, maybe electronic cohabitation even.

The Internet has always been about co-relating. Until the invention of the World Wide Web by a young British research scientist, Tim Berners-Lee, by far the most popular Internet feature was Usenet, the chat rooms, discussion groups, and community mobilizations that are still a main element of non-browser Internet conversations, showing up as alt.dot.something. America Online's success was largely built on its chat rooms, some fourteen thousand active ones at last count.

Now co-relations are just as much the currency of business as of the social and political domains of Web conversation. Communities of interest quickly swarm to and stay with co-relationship-centered sites. It's no surprise then that the Web sites of Fidelity, Schwab, and many other financial services providers are packed with ongoing seminars, chat groups, and tutorials. Conversation is what all this is about:

- When Fiat wanted to test some new design ideas for its Punto car, for example, it invited potential customers to select features for it on Fiat's Web site, in a process that Andersen Consulting calls "co-creation." Fiat tapped into a valuable source of information and feedback: three thousand car lovers responded to its request. "Co-creation adds a new dynamic to the producer/customer relationship by engaging customers directly in the production or distribution of value. Customers, in other words, can get involved at just about any stage of the value chain."[14]

- The CEO of Amazon summarized community as "the secret weapon of an online merchant."[15] Amazon.com is as much a community forum as a retailer. Amazon Associates, individuals and organizations that have their own Web sites targeted to their own communities, send business to Amazon. An Amazon executive commented that his company is not at all interested in, say, eighteenth-century muskets used by the Michigan militia, but there's a community out there that is and it wants books on the subject.
- CEO Tom Rielly of PlanetOut says, "It's not the content, it's the people, stupid. Content may be why people visit a site. But community is why they stay."[16]
- Garden Escapes began as an online nursery selling around three hundred types of plants. It was flooded with e-mailed questions and comments, so the owner of the company set up chat rooms and forums about regional gardening issues. The pattern of traffic shifted rapidly, with a doubling of average time per visit plus almost a doubling in average sale price. Business grew 40 percent a month. CEO Clifford A. Sharples says, "We thought of ourselves as more of a store. We underestimated how important community would be."[17]

A number of surveys show that people spend three times longer on sites that cater to chat visitors, and that adding this capability doubles traffic. Of course, that doesn't mean that it doubles sales and it may increase costs substantially.

The main draws to getting involved in an online community are, according to a *Business Week*/Harris poll, that it is related to work (42 percent), a social group (35 percent), or a hobby (18 percent).[18] Since the main source of revenues for most community sites is advertising, the pull is the extra time spent online. Geocities brings in $500,000 a month in ads and sponsorships; it hosts half a million free Web pages that it "arranges" as preferred communities, such as Restaurant Row (sponsored by Visa), Programmer's Pavilion (Microsoft), and Napa Valley (for wine lovers).

Marshall Industries has long been a leader in building customer relationships and communities online. Examples of its innovations include an electronic center for customers to design chips online and simulate their performance, regular network seminars that bring customers and experts together to discuss specialized topics, and an online chat facility for its engineering communities. One of these seminars brought together engineers from eighty-seven companies in twelve countries—and resulted in Marshall's selling several major development tools.

Communities can be small or large, personal or purely business. What they can't be—if they're to last—is artificial. They must fill a real need, as expressed by a volunteer chat host for AOL's Moms Online: "There is always someone who understands where you are coming from. This is my cyber neighborhood." They can take time to build and it's unclear how many of them will last in the longer term. As Howard Rheingold, author of *The Virtual Community,* put it, describing Sara Lee's efforts to establish a forum for its L'Eggs products: "Any company that thinks it can go out and create a community in 30 days is going to be disappointed. No matter what the type of neighborhood, it takes time, probably years, to build a lasting community."[19]

"Community," then, means a group with shared interests, identity, or affiliations. Community dominates the Internet, from chat rooms to the "market of one" customer segmentation that is the base for personalized service design to the many different types of portals that are the gravity creator that pulls people, groups, and businesses to a site. In business-to-business co-relations, the focus is increasingly on communities of mutual interest. Examples of community pull are plentiful:

- National Semiconductor customers need fast delivery of small volumes of components when their company's engineers are in the design stage of a new product, such as a cell phone or Web TV set top box. The "customer deals" described in Chapter Three benefit everyone—customers, distributors, and National Semi itself—and allow the company to tell within three months (rather than a year) if a new product is going to be a winner, just from the lead information.
- Most companies don't openly admit their products have bugs. In contrast, Cisco openly announces its bugs to the community of technical professionals who use its Web site. Site users solve around 4,500 problems a week for each other, even though they may be doing this for a competitor.

- Microsoft customizes its site to provide forums for individual communities to locate and interact with each other: CIOs, software developers, systems programmers, and many other distinct communities of interest.
- Yahoo's view is that it should make its Web site be like a person and also get the people it connects to hooked up to each other as well. If you do this, the value of your network increases immensely and at some point becomes self-sustaining. Yahoo is clearly well beyond this critical point, just as AOL is.

When it works, it works famously.

WHERE ONLINE RELATIONSHIPS MAY NOT WORK

The business model template for perfecting customer relationships is very powerful. Briefly put, it's very much the Wal-Mart business blueprint transferred from bricks and mortar to the online world. Indeed, many analysts are beginning to see Amazon as the new Wal-Mart. But it's important to recognize that there are only a few retailers in Wal-Mart's class and there will be only a few online equivalents. In addition, there will always be areas where the online interaction doesn't attract customers as fast or as much as expected. If you think of the Web as a *relationship* interface, you need to ask what the offline relationship interface is and what it provides. Take real estate, for example. The online opportunity is immense: house purchases amount to over a trillion dollars a year, around 15 percent of the economy. It's expensive and time-consuming. Agents take a high commission—typically 6–8 percent—for what appears to be a simple job. Storing and accessing listing information (including photographs, floor plans, information about the community) on the Web could save agents and buyers enormous amounts of time. (Sellers would save time too—they wouldn't need to clean or vacate their houses so often.) Logically, as many .coms thought, it ought to be a natural for Internet disintermediation of agents. The number of real estate Web sites grew from 3,000 to 250,000 between 1996 and 1999.

But to date, the online market has not taken off. First, the dealer community itself has a complex set of co-relationships. The purchase commission is split between the listing agent and the seller's agent. Should an agency move aggressively toward using an Internet listing service such as Microsoft Home Adviser and cut out local listing agents, how likely is it that next time—when it is the listing agent—the other parties will be eager to push its offers to their own clients?

In addition, even though many sellers of houses do indeed view the commission fee as very high and in many ways not justified by the value it provides, they need the co-relation help that a really good agent offers. That includes advice on whether or not to repaint the exterior, how to price the house, and setting up an open house for other agents. Buyers can easily save a lot of money via Web services, some of which exclude real estate agents; there are plenty of choices and plenty of benefits.[20] But in general, buyers and sellers stay with the co-relation provided by a good agent: help in picking the best local home inspector, information about comparable houses that have sold recently in the area, and patient listening to concerns.

Finally, there are the agents themselves. As with insurance and car selling, they have in general been wary of the Internet. As one observer comments, "They are, after all, salespeople, and as a rule salespeople are *people* people, not technology people." That can be interpreted as a negative—or a positive.

THE MANAGEMENT AGENDA: RELATIONSHIPS FOR THE FUTURE

As the transaction economy wears down and relationships more and more determine business success, the best relationship players will win out. The Web provides major advantages to some customers in some areas. Travel agents, car dealers, and insurance agents, for instance, now have to show that they can offer something over and above the online providers. It works the other way, too. Online players must show that they offer something the offline agents can't. Simply being a .com is not at all equivalent to being a skilled relationship innovator. In contrast, almost by definition, to be a .profit winner is to be a very skilled and committed relationship player.

The death of the transaction economy is inevitable. The rise of the relationship economy is also inevitable. Your company loses the relationship opportunity if it's just the end result of a search engine query. Establish yourself as a valued Internet brand so that customers park at your site as a matter of routine. Get your logistics in order so that you can afford to compete. Then drive every element of your organization toward the customer relationship. As we've discussed, that requires you to:

- Differentiate your offer through both time-tried and innovative methods. Get to the right pricing and be sure to follow up.
- Generate high repeat business. A starting point is to do something that in an offline world might seem heretical: help the customer shop with your competitors. Recognize that much of the Web's attraction for consumers and businesses is that it provides a wealth of information on options and an enormous range of choice. Make your firm contribute to that information and range rather than try to protect its proprietary space.
- Recognize that self-management of the relationship is the pivotal step in the path to value. This is how a company transforms its cost structures and its relationship base at the very same time. Every company that is a gorilla in Internet business has achieved this.
- Continue the customization and personalization that self-management begins. The interaction between customer and provider now goes way beyond standard transactions. The challenge is how far beyond this the company can move. For both the business-to-consumer and business-to-business market in the early .com era, everything was initially pretty standard—personal access but nonpersonal products and services. In .profit, *everything* is personal.
- Build collaboration and community everywhere. Once the customer comes to you and stays for reasons beyond just buying and searching for information, do as the exemplars do. Strengthen those bonds. Bring more and more to the relationship—more partners and more community focus.

If you have built and cultivated your long-term customer relationship, your firm will have the benefits of an extended relationship base. To multiply and broaden those benefits, continue progress on the path to value by harmonizing your channels—all on the customer's behalf.

7

HARMONIZE YOUR CHANNELS ON THE CUSTOMER'S BEHALF

Think like a customer, not a provider: there's no channel conflict, only channel choice.

Web business began with its being exploited as a very new and different channel, separate from traditional channels. That was the .com attitude. The .profit players see it differently—to them, it's part of the channel mix that best serves customer relationships.

Many well-known and well-respected businesses have shot themselves in the corporate foot by thinking about the Internet as a new channel. Manufacturers try to use the Web to compete with their established channels and are surprised that their retailers, dealers, and distributors are less than delighted. Insurance and real estate firms ignore the Internet because it's a tiny 1 percent factor in their marketplace and the existing broker channels offer so many face-to-face advantages. Companies that follow these paths justify what they are doing or not doing about the Internet as managing "channel conflict." Their efforts are misdirected.

It's worth reiterating: To the customer there's no such thing as channel conflict, only channel choice. Customers pick the provider that harmonizes its channels on their behalf instead of trying to control the channels to meet its own priorities and needs. Conventional wisdom has moved from the Internet's substituting "clicks" for "bricks and mortar" to "clicks and mortar" and even "mortar for clicks." That in no way means that firms have to be in all channels—bricks and mortar, call centers, distributors, and Internet. To do so would reflect as narrow a view as the old clicks versus bricks dichotomy. Instead, the real issue is that channel harmonization is an absolute priority.

Thus if your firm is an online player, it needs to consider where and why its customer relationships benefit from adding offline presence to .com, as many online leaders like AOL and Yahoo are doing by linking up with retailers like Wal-Mart and Kmart. If it's a hybrid, with both a traditional and an Internet operation, it needs to ensure the customer benefits from the interlinking, instead of their being in effect separate and even competing alternatives. If it is an established company moving online in pursuit of the benefits of direct sales, it needs to consider very carefully where its existing dealer system adds value to customers before trying to bypass that system and take the extra profit margin. And, of course, it must watch very carefully the online intermediaries, power brands, and relationship leaders that may offer customers more ease of access and personal service than the company itself ever can.

The business goal for channel harmonization is easy to state:

Make all your channels work together on behalf of the customers, so that you and they derive the most benefit from "clicks and mortar"—not Web or call center or physical location. Leverage face-to-face, voice-to-voice, and remote interaction. Focus your attention—and that of your channel partners—on meeting customer needs rather than addressing channel conflict.

If you don't get all this right, your firm is in deep, deep trouble; it has messed up customer relationships, distribution and sales, and cost management. Without those, what will keep it afloat?

CHANNEL OPTIONS: CHOICE, NOT CONFLICT

A major difference in management thinking between .com and .profit in Internet business surrounds the entire issue of channels—physical stores versus online Web sites, disintermediation of distributors, wholesalers, and even retailers that are a manufacturer's customers, prioritization of channels and channel relationships, and concerns about channel conflict. Channels serve two purposes:

- Add value to the customers in the link between the company's products and service offers and their own buying.
- Provide the best means of managing the logistics and support for all the processes that link producers to customers—manufacturers, retailers, and service providers, for example.

Almost by definition, the .com viewpoint is that the online channel is the best option for both customer and company, so that there is a conflict between it and other channels.

Channel conflict was one of the early .com watchwords, when the business focus was on using the Web to displace "bricks and mortar." Enthusiasts saw the Internet as taking over just about everything, dooming the operators of physical businesses. Even in 2000, the .com sense of certainty remained surprisingly prevalent. Consider the following short extracts from a fourteen-page article in *PC Computing* titled "The Internet Is Crushing Whole Industries. . . . Is Your Company Next?":

> These people [travel agent, broker, and insurance sales rep] are toast. . . .
> No doubt about it, your local car dealer's showroom will eventually become a wholesaler's warehouse. . . . Companies that stand to gain everything from moving to the Internet (and risk everything by keeping their pricey storefronts) shouldn't wait. . . . [It's] downtown retailers and superstores that have tags on their toes.[1]

That's about as assertive a statement of the .com position as you'll find. If you accept it, then your existing channel partners are indeed toast, and your firm should dump them fast. Obviously, every channel player now has to look at online alternatives as a potential competitor because of the Internet value drivers. If the Web provides for better relationship value, logistics value, power brand value, and intermediary value, customers will choose it, without doubt.

Insurance and real estate agents have worried that online players would end run them to get to their customers. So far, they have been delighted that the value calculus still favors them. Car dealers and retailers have worried that large manufacturers would muscle their way into their market at their expense—that a General Motors would start selling its cars directly to customers or a Levi Strauss restrict its retailers' Web offers and activities in order to make hay in the Internet sunshine. That has happened, but with mixed results. Levi's party got very heavily rained on. The car companies are gearing up their Internet efforts. There's quite a lot of jousting between dealers and manufacturers. The dealers are under pressure but not yet under siege. They are using legal and political leverage to require that every sale be finalized via a dealer.

Business thinking has shifted from the either-or of channel conflict to the both-and of channel harmony. *PC Computing*'s underlying assumption is that the auto industry won't make adjustments to ensure the dealerships are part of the customer value equation. .Profit assumes that, for instance, the carmakers will use online Web channels to inform the customer about products, build a relationship with car owners, and strengthen the dealers' position through referrals, help in configuring options, scheduling maintenance, and maintaining historical service information about a car purchased from the dealer. If travel agents, brokers, and insurance reps just continue the practices of today, they will be toast. But the best, the forward-thinking ones—they will be making bread instead.

Combining Channels, with a Plan

Although there are plenty of purely online players such as eBay and Amazon, the general new priority across businesses is to combine the best of online and offline operations. It's no longer a matter of either-or but of the best combination. This is especially so in retailing, as some recent moves by both click companies and chains illustrate:

- AOL, the "clicks" giant, reached a deal with "old-fashioned retailer" Circuit City that will help AOL reach a broader market and gain from the selling of wireless devices in the "bricks" stores. AOL gets dedicated space in 615 Circuit City stores.[2] The day after this announcement,

AOL made a deal with Wal-Mart to co-offer Internet access through Wal-Mart's stores.

- Microsoft has already made a similar arrangement with Radio Shack that offers mutual tie-ups for Internet access, wireless, portable personal computers, Internet television, and whatever else the telecommunications and consumer electronics revolution next generates.

- Yahoo has linked up with Kmart to create a new Internet access service, Bluelight.com, named after the well-known Kmart blue light special. The service will be accessed through a special Yahoo page that is co-branded with Kmart.

- Egghead, a failing "bricks" seller of computer hardware and software, closed all of its stores and went totally online. It soon turned itself around in terms of both revenues and profits.

- Gateway, a successful "clicks" retailer of personal computers, went in the opposite direction, adding physical marketing and service centers to encourage a more personal and direct link with customers and potential buyers.

- Sears continues to focus on its stores but is seeing benefits from small-scale online operations that enhance the physical ones by, for instance, offering convenience in processing credit card applications and pick-up of goods.

- Homepoint.com, which began as a straight online operation, decided not to compete directly against furniture stores but instead uses links to them as fulfillment and distribution centers.

What's most noteworthy about these examples is the variety of strategies and collaborations they indicate. Old-fashioned retailers are wooing and being wooed by the most "virtual" companies. Online firms are building up off-line presence and the reverse. All this may possibly reflect some confusion—if no one really knows what's best to do, then there's turmoil, try-it-and-see, and hedging of bets. More likely, though, is the simple reality that every channel offers something special *to the customer* and also has advantages and disadvantages for the business itself. The business model opportunity and challenge is to get the best mix of channel options *on behalf of the customer* that also leverages your firm's own economics, productivity, reputation, and business relationships. That is, the value imperative is channel harmony and the resulting business model is a clear channel management plan.

Eradicate Conflict

Get rid of the term *channel conflict*. It's the wrong viewpoint because it looks at channels from the perspective of the provider, not that of the customer. Customers respond to the best choices for themselves. They care about channel options; any channel conflict is your problem, not theirs. But this is a hard lesson, a big shift.

There has been—and continues to be—plenty of discussion of channel conflict in the business and Internet trade press. Where does the use of the Net as a primary channel cannibalize your own sales or threaten your distributors? Where does your distribution system become a liability to you? When do you want to sell directly to the end customer, making you in effect a competitor with your distributors? The very tone of these questions suggests conflict and implies a zero-sum game: my win is your loss and the reverse.

There are certainly situations in which zero-sum may apply—but there's growing evidence that if you think in terms not of "your" channels but of the customer relationship and the partnerships that support that relationship, then you can create a win-win situation through channel harmony.

Optimize Options

With channel harmony, the issue of distributors becomes one not of zero-sum but of ways to make relationships and collaborations with distributors optimize customer options. It may well be, for example, that in real estate most home buyers will always prefer to use an agent. In that case, effective business models for channel harmony will include the agents as a key part of the strategic equation—they will not try to disintermediate them but to complement them. Those models will include referrals, for example, and providing information hubs and services to agents. One of the payoffs to real estate agents in encouraging the growth of sites that provide a new information channel to home buyers is the opportunity to look at houses online without setting up an appointment to visit them. Typically, people take a drive to look at around a dozen houses before settling on the one they want. That figure is at least halved through the Internet, which not only saves the customer time but greatly reduces the agent's workload in setting up appointments and accompanying potential buyers.

But just because such a business model accepts the likelihood of the existing channel and distribution system's remaining the largest force in an industry—real estate dealers, retail stores, car dealers, and insurance agents, for instance—that does not mean that treating the Web as a threat or ignoring it should be part of the plan. That seems to be a commonplace view among agents and dealers. They'll have to adjust and include the Internet in their own business models—or they'll surely be gone within a few years, proving the *PC Computing* prophecy even though it was by no means inescapable when it was made.

Be Alert to Change

The travel agency business offers a warning signal here. For decades, the agents had tight control of the customer relationship and were at the center of the airline-to-customer channel system. Even with airlines owning the reservation systems travel agents used and with customers having the option to book via the carrier, the agency system held firm. When American Airlines first tried to introduce electronic tickets, the agents squashed the plan by threatening to pick other airlines' flights where those met the passenger's requirements. In the 1980s, commissions averaged 10 percent of the fare with generous "overrides" as incentives for volume. Deregulation of the industry and the growth of airline reservation systems led to an increase and not a decrease in agents' share of bookings, to around 80 percent of all tickets.

That has changed completely. These days, smaller agents are losing sales fast and many are going out of business. The airlines have been able to cut their commissions to a maximum of $50 a ticket. Customers have responded strongly to the new Internet channels. Expedia, Travelocity, and other online services provide lower fares and sophisticated, convenient, and easy-to-use tools for searching for the best deals and configuring complex travel schedules.

Airlines also offer first-rate personalized sites. American Airlines, for instance, has created a new dialogue with its frequent flyers, by definition the most profitable and loyal of its customers. The target community for its Web initiative was the 87 percent of the 32 million participants in its AAdvantage program who had a computer at home. Of these customers, 70 percent reported that they would like to do business with American Airlines electronically, on their own time, when it best suited them, which was likely to be at night or on weekends. For their business travel, these customers rely on their company travel department. American found, somewhat to its surprise, that they immediately welcomed interactive e-mail, such as offers of "specials." In the first month, 20,000 signed up—and the total jumped to 800,000 in a year. In 1999, there were close to 2 million subscribers using this online self-management capability. American Airlines allows members to specify their own "business rules"—such as "automatically inform me about fares under $400 to any of the following beach destinations in December and January." Recent releases of the site provide additional personalization: profiling and preference information (meals, seat location, and so on), addition of up to ten other linked profiles, plus multiple credit cards with labels (Business, Pleasure).

This makes the airlines' own Web site offerings a new channel that bypasses agents and it clearly threatens the future of all except those that can establish a strong relationship base. The standard travel agency has little to offer that a customer can't choose to get elsewhere. It breaks up the almost symbiotic relationship between agents and airlines. For decades the agents held the power; now they don't. Log onto the American Airlines or Lufthansa site and you can get tailored deals that few agents could routinely and regularly track for you.

Another type of new channel is represented by Priceline.com, which has grabbed a sizable share of the consumer market for travel through its patented pricing software. Individuals state the price they are willing to pay to travel to a given destination on a given day. If an airline is willing to accept this offer, Priceline confirms the deal. There are some complicated and sometimes controversial aspects of how this all works. For instance, under Priceline's system, the price you name is legally binding. You have to take the offered deal, which may take you from Washington to Las Vegas with a four-hour stopover in Kansas City, departing at 1:20 A.M., but with the $120 price you required. Priceline is buying block seats from airlines such as Delta, so that technically consumers could locate as good or as better a deal by themselves. But that was true with travel agents. Price-line is a new channel that attracts bargain hunters and is more convenient than searching the Web. It's hard to find a label for Priceline. It's not part of the established channel structures. It's neither agent nor distributor nor provider.

So travel agents are being squeezed. They were the key intermediary between provider and customer. They'd been able to maintain that role for decades. They're upset. They can be as upset as they please. Customers are shifting, not in droves but at a pace fast enough and a rate big enough to change the rules of the competitive game. (At the start of 2000, most estimates were that 3 percent of all tickets were booked directly through a Web site.) It's no use complaining that it's unfair. Whenever a company talks about channel conflict, either as manufacturer, distributor, or seller, that means basically "it's unfair to me" when one of the players uses the Internet to move into its established business base and "mine, mine" when the company itself is trying to do this.

That's channel conflict and it ignores the Internet relationship reality that the customer will decide. In an article headlined "Retailers' Resentment Grows with Online Sales," *USA Today* provides a detailed "unfair to me" review of furniture retailers plus a "mine, mine" commentary on furniture manufacturers:

> Manufacturers are in a painful evaluation of the desire to sell online vs. the practical wisdom of maintaining their existing channel of distribution through retailers. . . .
>
> Indeed, some furniture executives dismiss virtual retail, citing delivery concerns, service demands, and the high risk of alienating retailers.
>
> Others believe it is here to stay because consumers have shown a strong willingness to shop online.
>
> Retailers have responded to [online companies'] price reductions by leveraging their buying power against suppliers. Merchants are telling manufacturers that serving the renegade "furniture-something-dot-com-mies" constitutes mercantile treason. The sentence is immediate death in the form of dissolving their relationships.[3]

There's some interesting language here that might keep a therapist in business for quite some time. *Mercantile treason, painful evaluation, dot-commies* (a neat turn of phrase!), *resentment, renegades, immediate death.* All this discussion is clearly very much about conflict. And it's all pretty self-defeating. The customer, not the combatants, will decide the winner. The article describes Furniture.com—commie?—a standout company in terms of service and price, and one that creates channel harmony instead of channel warfare. It offers a personal adviser online, excellent telephone service, a choice of over 50,000 items in its showroom (obviously far more than any store could offer), and a 15–25 percent discount relative to retail prices. Customers rate it very highly in terms of all the criteria of quality and service for both online and offline retailing.

One final extract from the *USA Today* article contrasts with the point quoted earlier about consumers displaying a "strong willingness" to shop online:

> [A manufacturer] found out that retailers were serious. Their executives ran a test on Living.com in July. "We did it for two weeks but received a real negative response from retailers. They thought we were bypassing them. . . . From there we said, 'Don't disturb the nucleus of our retailers for a really small part of the market.'"

This view of channels is surely self-defeating. How about the customer? If customers do indeed develop a strong willingness to shop online, this attitude amounts to "we won't let them." But customers will ignore that and go online anyway. How about a different approach? How about ensuring that whatever channels customers prefer to use, you—the retailer, the manufacturer, or the distributor—are part of the *customer's* value equation?

There are plenty of companies that think this way. They are counters to the *PC Computing* claims and very much a combination of value-driven thinking—customer relationship, logistics, and brand. A few examples:

• Even though it's been selling online since 1992 (a deal with America Online) and has had its own Web site since 1995, 1-800-FLOWERS receives only 15 percent of its orders online. "A lot of people browse through the selections online but purchase using the telephone," one executive notes, adding, "Or they make an online purchase but follow up over the phone with questions about delivery. And customers want a consistent shopping experience, whether they log onto a Web site, call in an order, or walk into a store."[4] 1-800-FLOWERS sees the call center and Web as a unified single channel, not separate ones.

• Sony uses its Web site (hosted on GE's TPN) to strengthen its own relationships with consumers and business customers without weakening its distributors. It uses the interaction and information it gathers to assess which type of channel partner it should refer the sale to—retailer, systems integrator, OEM, or reseller. This form of prequalification of prospects obviously helps the distributor retain the direct customer link while Sony at the same time uses the Web interaction and data it gathers to increase its sales. "We are a channel marketing group. Our relationships and partnerships are so important and this Web site will enhance our ability to work with our partners." Previously, the Web site was product-focused and tried to speak to too many customer segments at the same time. Telemarketing was the main source of leads, though costly. Now, the updated site enables "needs-based" navigation and delivers a customer to the right distributor. Sony's aim is to "keep the sanctity of the distribution network."

• An interview with Charles Schwab's director of corporate communications captures its operating philosophy: "Our research shows that about half of our 4.9 million customers have visited one of our offices. And the fraction is higher for our more affluent customers. People want to feel close to their money—branch offices provide that. They also want to meet brokers and bounce ideas off them. And sometimes they need to pick up a check within a few hours. For all these reasons, we have strong incentives to keep our storefront a vital part of our services. So for us, online versus storefront is not a conflict. It is part of a mix of services that our customers are quickly getting used to. The mix is actually larger—customers also get 24-hour telephone access to humans as well as to speech-recognition and touch-tone telephone services. . . . We are always improving our personalization efforts."

• Fruit of the Loom represents the most proactive approach to channel harmonization. Many of its direct customers are small businesses that produce customized T-shirts or that sell through catalogs. Fruit of the Loom provides them with free Web site development and hosting and even allows them to offer goods from competitors such as Haynes. The logic is that by strengthening the quality of the seller's Web presence—including ensuring quality of design—Fruit of the Loom gains in both the distributor relationship and the customer relationship. "We decided our partners were our best bet for Web business."

Fruit of the Loom also links them to its own Web site, which acts as a product locator for the distributors' customers—companies that buy T-shirts in bulk and customize or embellish them. For instance, a customer may want 10,000 extra large blue T-shirts to print up and sell at, say, a rock concert. "He just logs on, puts in his product request and zip code and I give him the nearest distributor. Yeah, I've spent a lot of money setting this up, but I've put 10,000 Fruit of the Loom T-shirts in front of my distributor's customer with no marketing effort." The reported benefits include a reduction in order delivery time from between three and five days to overnight, savings in processing costs for the distributor of $10–$20 per order—significant in this low-margin business—and increased sales of as much as 25 percent. Fruit of the Loom also benefits from each roughly $100,000 customized site since the distributor prominently displays the company's own logo, strengthening brand awareness of Fruit of the Loom among its own customer base. In addition, the feature that permits distributors to advertise and sell competitors' products online automatically offers a Fruit of the Loom equivalent if the item is out of stock.[5]

(A cautionary note must be added here. When your core business strategy isn't working, an Internet add-on won't save the situation. At the end of 1999, Fruit of the Loom was in deep financial trouble. It had lost $166 million on $548 million in sales.)

Adjust Distribution for Harmony, Not Discord

Distribution channels are part of a company's basics. They are at the core of most relationships, processes, and operations. It's thus hard to see how companies like Levi Strauss and Herman Miller expected to gain by explicitly trying to take out their channel partners—channel partners that do offer real value to the customer. Levi started selling Dockers and jeans over the Net, while refusing to allow retailers to sell online. In addition, it offered some special items that could be bought only via Levi's own site: the retailers couldn't order the goods for their stores. Retailers like Macy's and J.C. Penney had to pressure Levi to get permission to add Levi's products to their own online offers. Very quickly, Levi thought better of trying to keep the cybermarket to itself. It quit direct sales on the Web and left online selling of its clothing to retailers. As *Computerworld* put it, "Levi's is a perfect example of a manufacturer realizing it didn't have the channel power it thought it would on the Web."[6]

For Levi, using the Web to cut out the middleman turns out to have a deep downside. Others found the same results:

• Herman Miller went even further than Levi Strauss in disenfranchising its distributors by promising to undercut *any* price that its own channel "partners" offer. This makes little sense, especially since so much of the customer relationship rests on the local presence of the company that will handle delivery and assembly of the expensive and complex Herman Miller chairs and carry out repairs, reupholstering, and whatnot. One of its distributors removed any mention of the company from its own Web sites. Herman Miller entirely revamped the business model for its online initiatives and is now a model for logistics integration and customer service.

• Gibson Musical Instruments announced it would sell its guitars over its Web site at 10 percent below list price. "The dealers were irate. We took them off before we sold any."[7] It then decided to compromise and limit online sales to strings and accessories. The dealers remain less than ecstatic. The underlying question: "Why have dealers if you're going retail?"

Fundamentally, the issues of channel strategies have to be looked at from the perspective of the customer. Where is the relationship interface and what value does it provide to the customer? If the channel relationship is bypassed or augmented, will extra value be created along the entire manufacturer-to-purchaser chain? Will that value be lasting? There are lessons in harmony from the leaders.

THE MANAGEMENT AGENDA: CHANNELS FOR THE CUSTOMER

Dell, as always the process innovator of our time, brilliantly meshes all its channels on behalf of the customer. One Dell innovation that many companies appear to be adopting is software that simply and even automatically routes the customer between channels. For example, if a Web user has problems with getting answers to frequently asked questions (FAQs) or in configuration and trouble-shooting, an option on the screen (a telephone icon) directly links the customer to a technical specialist whose own screen shows the very same script the customer is working with. Schwab's Web site, also designed with the customer in mind, ensures that any breakdown in Web service immediately switches the customer to a human sales rep. Dell and Schwab present a single company image. This is very much the direction channel management thinking is moving: the customer should never be aware of "channels."

In contrast, many companies try to blend a new business model (direct selling and service relationship with the customer) with the old (third parties as the direct link). In this, they still rely on distributors—while positioning to bypass them. The most notorious example is Compaq, which in mid-1999 announced its first quarterly loss of the decade. Compaq's channel costs are far higher than Dell's. (As noted earlier, Dell's cost edge is around 15 percent; it turns its inventory over sixty times a year, versus Compaq's seven or eight times, and so on.) Compaq's channel structure is more expensive than Dell's and makes the company very much dependent on the strength of its distributor relationships. When Compaq acquired Digital, it tried to blend direct selling with its own and Digital's OEM (original equipment manufacturer) channels. Its foray into direct PC sales was, not surprisingly, less than enthusiastically received by its distributors. Compaq's business model began to show fractures, almost to the point of full disintegration.

All Dell's main competitors—IBM, Hewlett-Packard, and Compaq—have had to adapt their channel strategies to include selling direct instead of only through distributors and resellers. Hewlett-Packard has faced the same margin pressures as Compaq. The difference is that it has strong channel relationships—to the extent that it's known as "the channel's best friend."

Compaq tried to act as if bypassing its dealers was no big deal, but of course the dealers were not fooled. Hewlett-Packard didn't try to fool them. Its strategy is a combination of the three that seem to be emerging as business models for channel harmonization. These are the options for the management agenda:

- Unify the customer relationship through multichannel access. This is the Dell and Schwab approach.
- Provide a value-added service to distributors by acting as a gateway for customers to be best matched to distributors, resellers, and systems integrators. This is Sony's strategy.
- Use the company's Web presence to strengthen the channel partners. Fruit of the Loom is an exemplar here.

Which is best for you? There's no simple answer to how to build an effective business model for channel harmony. Channel management is complex, made especially so by the very fact that we are in the transitional stage between "electronic" and "commerce." So, for instance, you can make a case either way that real estate will inevitably move to primarily electronic service via the Internet or that it will just as inevitably remain primarily based on personal and face-to-face service, with the Internet a secondary factor. You could argue the same for most aspects of retailing, car dealerships, insurance, and other areas of business where today the primary contact with the customer is not the manufacturer of the product or the creator of the service but an agent or distributor. What will the customer of tomorrow want and expect? That depends. How soon is "tomorrow"?

We can't point to the most effective business model for your channel strategies. But we can stress that channel harmony is a value imperative. It's more and more clear that in many instances the channel *is* the customer relationship. So start with the customer and work back through the channel options and opportunities you may find for your firm in the channel structures. Don't go the other way round—and don't just tinker around. Achieving channel harmony is truly imperative. You can't successfully move on to the other imperatives without it.

8

BUILD A POWER BRAND FOR YOUR BUSINESS

Brands have power—and take power. Internet relationship brands are killing off product brand equity.

Amazon, Yahoo, and AOL have built the same degree of brand name recognition across the world as Nike, Coca Cola, and IBM. They are among the Internet power brands that are contributing to the death of product brand equity. When you're a loyal repeat buyer on your personalized MyXYZ site, XYZ is the brand, whatever products you buy there.

The Internet business shakeout will result in a few power brands and plenty of niche players with their own strong brands. The question is, Which brands and which players? When the deregulation of airlines initially led to a flood of new entrants with high promise and high expectations and then industry consolidation reduced the competition to a handful of megabrands, there were plenty of surprises. A few of the new companies stayed in business—Southwest Airlines being the Amazon equivalent (and a major .profit player, with the highest percentage in the industry of reservations made through its Web site). Some well-established players such as Eastern Airlines and Pan Am were gone and soon forgotten.

Today's battle to become a portal is really about branding for a new economy. If you're not an Internet power brand, how do you differentiate yourself and stay visible? What do you do when your strong offline product brand has no value in the online world? You can't have a business model without having a branding strategy. Saying that your firm is going to be a portal may look great in the press announcement, but it's like saying it's going to be a brand. Customers make brands. Customers make portals. What value are you offering that will get those customers to turn your firm into their brand value? Your company can call itself anything it wants, but unless customers view your site as somewhere to go on a routine basis, all you'll have will be a .com Web site.

Here's the power brand business goal:

Build a brand that attracts customers to routinely "park" at your site, and then add more and more reasons for them to come back rather than surf or search elsewhere. Turn the brand into your online market complex and the platform for a sustained stream of innovations.

The most exciting, volatile, and controversial business model template refers to the one that is all about building power in the new marketplace today to ensure massive power for tomorrow. It's the Yahoomazon game—trying to become the electronic Wal-Mart, loved by customers, feared by competitors, and wooed by suppliers. It's also the one with most hype attached because the stakes and risks are so high—for company and investors. And they're high for competitors, of course. The business model is simple in essence: build a powerful brand that you can use in any way that makes sense. Through e-services, you can quickly and seamlessly add other people's services to your site.

THE POWER OF E

Craigg Ballance, a principal in Canada's E-Finity, a firm that provides end-to-end services for .profit companies (and a close friend of Peter Keen and coauthor with him of three books on electronic business), captures the implications of this by taking "power" literally. He talks not about e-something, but of business to the power of e: plain business, or business squared, cubed, and to the fourth power. He makes the point that "e" doesn't stand for "electronic" but for excellence, ecosystem, enterprise—take your pick about the item you want to raise to the next power. (He also amusingly describes Canadian Internet business as Eh! commerce.)

Ballance's terminology of powers of e provides a helpful way of getting across the ambition of the business model template for building a power brand. E^1—e to the power of 1—is business as is. The goal of .com was to raise it to the power of 2—to square it. That's the ambition of the many companies that have a strong Web presence, bulletproof transaction platforms, and sensible value paths ahead. E^3 is what our book is all about—the most aggressive .profit business model templates. And e^4 is the Big Enchilada—a dominant power position on the Internet as the Internet moves into the mainstream of all business—and in some instances becomes the mainstream and crowds other business models out.

Amazon is, of course, the poster child. Here's just one power play it made on September 29, 1999:

> Today, Amazon announced the introduction of three new innovations: "z.Shops," "Amazon.com Payments," and "All Products Search." With these moves Amazon is harnessing the Internet to change the game entirely. . . .
>
> z.Shops: Amazon will allow anyone who wants to sell anything to list it on Amazon's site and sell it to Amazon's large, 10 million plus audience. It makes it very easy for anyone to set up an e-commerce business. Sellers will pay $9.99 a month for Web space on Amazon.com to sell up to 3,000 unique items. . . . Amazon has created a virtual marketplace. It won't be taking any inventory of the products being sold. Like eBay, it will be able to generate huge gross margins on the products being sold. . . . Starting tomorrow, more than 500,000 new items will be available on Amazon.com. . . .
>
> Amazon.com Payments: This will enable easy payment between buyer and seller. It will allow individuals and small businesses to accept payments through Amazon.com's 1-click feature . . . your credit card information is held by Amazon, which eliminates the need to enter that information each time you make a purchase. . . .
>
> All Products Search: This feature will help shoppers find anything for sale on the Internet, not just on Amazon.[1]

Amazon may or may not succeed in creating this virtual marketplace—though solving the payment-handling problem, one of the biggest difficulties for individuals and small businesses, will certainly help—but in any case it demonstrates the power of e at work. Very few players in Internet business could bring this off. Clearly, the standard .com doesn't have the customer base and relationships, the collaborations, or the technology platform. Middle-of-the-road online players don't have the brand and all the credibility that's required: trust, comfort, familiarity, and marketing reach.

One of the most unique aspects of the Internet, once you have the brand to exploit the relationship opportunity—or perhaps it's the other way around—is that it makes diversification natural and easy in a way that a new extension of business can co-relate well with existing business. Amazon's founder has said again and again that he never thought of Amazon as a book retailer; that was just a starting point. What's the ending point? Amazon, like other power brand builders, destroys the concept of an "industry" that has been fundamental to management thinking for over a century. At the very same time *and through the very same relationship interface* Amazon is a retailer, an auction house, a medical supplier, a catalog retailer, and now a new style of bank and a business hub.

Of course, Amazon may overstretch itself and, like most of the conglomerates of the 1970s, find that the parts don't fit together. But, like Jack Welch's General Electric, it may create a company of extraordinary diversified cohesion. We do not have any industry labels to put on an Amazon, an AOL, a Dell, a Schwab, or a Yahoo. Dell's now in auctions. Schwab's into just about everything to do with finance. That makes the power brands destructive as well as constructive. As they construct their power of e, they intrude into the territory of offline firms—and many successful online players. Amazon's extensions of its business have already affected the position of CD Now (CDs), and eBay (auctions). The announcements we've quoted will affect AOL, Yahoo, online banks and malls, and search engines. It really helps when you already have Internet brand equity.

GORILLA POWER: INCREASING RETURNS

Geoffrey Moore (coauthor of *The Gorilla Game*) has aptly explained much of the high value that very skilled investors place on stocks of companies that take a clear lead in an ecosystem. His argument runs as follows:

> When a new competitive ecosystem emerges, there will be many
> players in it, some new and some established. No one knows who the

winner will be, so once it's clear that this is a hypergrowth area of innovation it makes sense for an investor to choose a variety of stocks to bet on. But if one of the competitors becomes a gorilla, the dominant pacesetter in the ecosystem, the new brand name, and the market leader, and leaves the rest to roam around as chimpanzees, then the rule is simple: dump them and keep the gorilla. It's not that the chimps won't make money but they will only make the money that their size and place in the ecosystem permits.[2]

Cisco has been a strong company from its early days as the inventor of the router hardware that linked previously incompatible local area networks. In the past few years, it has raced ahead of its main competitors—and it is now a gorilla. It has lavished attention on the imperatives: it has grown its revenues, integrated its logistics base, and built strong customer relationships much faster than its competitors. The market rewarded it by bidding up the total value of the company to close to a trillion dollars—many times that of the next six players in Cisco's mainstream business ecosystem *combined*. Cisco is throwing its weight around by using its market e[4] power to make acquisitions and launch innovations through the *people* in the forty companies it has acquired in the past six years. Gorillas use financial capital to gain intellectual capital. When Cisco acquired Cerent in late 1999, it paid $6.9 billion for a tiny company with around $10 million in revenues. Asked what was the basis for the firm's valuation of Cerent, its CEO, John Chambers, answered "Two million dollars an engineer."

The Gorilla Game reflects a complex recent shift in economic thought, called "increasing returns." This basically means that to those that have, more will be given—and more will be taken from those that have not. Traditional microeconomics insisted that the nature of markets and prices meant decreasing returns. As the market grew and matured, the demand and supply curves intersected, with smaller and smaller payoffs—diminishing marginal returns—to all the players. This traditional model fits well with the economics of manufacturing but has been revealed as the very opposite of the information technology industry.

An example of increasing returns is Microsoft. In its early years, Microsoft was just one of a half dozen companies competing in the operating systems wars. Operating systems like CP/M and Pascal disappeared as Microsoft's DOS gained market share, greatly aided by IBM's adopting it for its personal computers. Unix looked like a winner, especially since it was the base for the computer components of the early Internet. At any stage in this early development—a sort of Operating Systems War of the Acronyms—Microsoft was not the obvious winner.

Once it became so and established its previously second-rate and second-place Windows as *the* personal computer operating system, it crowded out everybody, most obviously IBM, whose OS/2 was in many ways superior. It started to crowd out Apple, whose OS was very clearly superior. Those superiorities quickly became irrelevancies. For years, developers of software in the graphics design field and desktop publishing had built their products for Apple first and then for Microsoft Windows. As Windows achieved dominance, both software and hardware providers built their wares for Microsoft first, which reduced costs as competition increased for printers, scanners, software packages, and telecommunications add-ons. That gave Microsoft an even bigger lead over Apple, which in turn pushed the industry to build its products to the Microsoft standards and systems, which in turn gave Microsoft an even bigger lead. And so on. Apple still survives—though it has had several near-death experiences—and it should continue to do well in its niche areas, but it's a chimpanzee and not a gorilla.

One commentator points out that the gorillas become the brand that new customers pick, so that even when a competitor has a large and loyal customer base, it's on the way to becoming a chimp. That's very much what happened to Apple. There are many writers for whom there is no choice but the Apple Powerbook G3. Apple's iMac machines, announced in late 1998, have been a big hit. But Apple is still a chimp—albeit a large one. It's loved by the many writers and designers who use its products, but when the Microsoft gorilla walks through the undergrowth, the chimp can only scamper away.

BRAND BATTLES

The .com phase of the Internet was basically about which companies could become gorillas. Amazon, Dell, and Cisco are very big gorillas. Wal-Mart was the gorilla of its era and remains one today. It's very likely to wander on over to the Internet space, thump its chest, and show that first mover advantage may not matter quite as much as .com zealots have thought. Wal-Mart's executives have made the point many times that they saw no reason to join the rush to be a .com. Rushing wouldn't make good use of its relationship strengths, its stores, or its brand. Instead, Wal-Mart chose HP to help build its new site, which develops all these. Wal-Mart waited until early January 2000 to relaunch its previously very limited Web site, after making deals with AOL and Gateway, the consumer PC retailer. The Wal-Mart gorilla is on the move.

Of course, even gorillas can lose their way or be beaten up and an even bigger beast take over their place in the competitive food chain. That might happen to Amazon. It did happen to Kmart, the gorilla that Wal-Mart displaced. There can be only a few gorillas in an ecosystem. That's why the market is willing to place a premium on newcomers—on baby gorillas—that look like they have the ability to take over the territory, even when they are small and unprofitable. An example is eToys, an online retailer whose total 1998 sales were $30 million—less than Toys "R" Us sold in just two of its 1,500 bricks-and-mortar stores. Yet the market valued the online baby gorilla far higher than the venerable store chain.

The two firms fought a well-publicized battle for sales over the 1999 Christmas period. That battle showed both the power of branding and the limits of .com. Toys "R" Us attracted more hits than any retailer except Amazon. That suggests that an offline brand can transfer to the Web. However, this was just a .com, in that the company handled many aspects of logistics and relationships poorly, with frequent reports about orders not being delivered on time and customers not being told that goods were backlisted or out of stock. This adds to brand erosion, not brand building. eToys did a much better job. A survey of customer satisfaction over the Christmas sales period shows that eToys scored an average of 7.9 on a 10-point scale and Toys "R" Us 7.04.[3] Both companies were in the top five online sites in terms of sales. Toys "R" Us looks like it is fighting back and eToys faces its own problems as the market questions its .profit potential.

The future of Internet business rests with the gorillas. It's as simple as that. The power brands determine the direction of the online economy and, increasingly, the economy. The baby gorillas are the innovators of today; some will become the new gorillas.

Every other company—every non-gorilla—is left in a niche position. This can be as satisfying and profitable as, say, your favorite restaurant or specialty store (including a bookstore). But as the power brands intrude into other industries they weaken the branding and relationship power of many product companies (what publisher now has the name recognition and draw of Amazon?) and their portals command premium positions that translate into premium fees for others to be a spoke on their hub. As discussed in Chapter Three, the fees other companies pay to have a presence on a power brand portal are directly analogous to ads on network television. Even now, when ABC, CBS, and NBC are not the network giants they once were (they clearly are not gorillas and the market doesn't pay a premium for their stock), they still have a commanding position in many areas, as shown by the advertising fees for thirty-second slots on the Super Bowl broadcast.

The power of brand explains how Yahoo turned a free information service into a cash flow machine. Companies pay it and AOL millions to be on their branded site. For example:

- eToys pays AOL a $3 million annual fee and offers 35 percent of the sales price to any Web site that steers a customer to its own site.
- First USA has made two five-year deals, one with AOL for $50 million and one with Microsoft Network for $90 million.
- Beyond.com's 1999 first quarter revenues were $19.1 million. Its three-year deal with AOL (made in 1998) was for $21 million, and that with Excite.com was $4.9 million, also for three years.[4]

These make for high marketing costs—and the payments may well be worth it. AOL claims that 8 percent of all online purchases come from referrals and links from its own site. But they certainly change the steepness of the path to .profit. Preview Travel lost $5.5 million in the first quarter of 1999, two years into a $55.5 million deal with AOL. It reported then that it was facing serious financial problems, and that it might not be able to meet its contractual obligations to AOL. Meanwhile, AOL itself, a company that was written off many times over the past decade, thrives. It generated a billion dollars of positive cash flow on its 1999 revenues of $4.8 billion. (Rupert Murdoch didn't take up an opportunity to buy into AOL, partly because his good friend Bill Gates, at the time a skeptic about the

Internet's business potential, told him that AOL would be dead by the next Christmas.)

PREDICTING THE WINNERS

Our discussion of AOL highlights the obvious: no one knows which firm will become a gorilla power brand. But this business model highlights a key element in the .profit agenda: whether online or offline, today's business is really all about brands. For online players, the question is, What happens to your brand if you're six clicks down on AOL's site or just a lucky hit via a search engine? For offline players, the question is, What is your brand now and what must you do to maintain its value in a world where online brands offer special value?

We don't have a secret formula for making a power brand in the .profit era. Nor does anyone else. It's like predicting Wal-Mart's future when it had ten stores, or predicting which of the many rapidly growing business-to-business trading hubs that are baby gorillas will grow up to full size. What we do reliably know is that not one of the power brands became one via .com thinking. We see too many companies talking about their own power brand ambitions in .com terms. In the early euphoria of Internet business, too many large companies assumed that their existing brand would transfer easily, if expensively, to the Net. Now, too many seem to assume that *portal* means *Web site* and that all they need is the right design and right designer of the site. No, no, no, and no.

It's neither a formula nor a guarantee, but here is what we see as key for the management agenda:

- *Focus*. The power brands are remarkably focused in their priorities. The role model is General Electric; the keywords, cohesive diversity. Like GE, the power brands build their brand by knowing what they want it to be, so that all the very diverse collaborations, acquisitions, offers, and innovations that they enter into add up to brand power. Anything that doesn't is a brand distraction or a dilution. That's a very real problem for today's gorillas and a big opportunity for some baby gorillas wandering around out there now.

- *Market, market, market*. This is not an issue of advertising. It's getting the story out—making the business model visible and credible.

One of the main lessons to learn from the power brand builders is that marketing is a line function and a key element in mobilizing the organization and in building a market capitalization premium. AOL's marketing drew attention to its strengths of convenience, ease of use, and wide availability and away from its many weaknesses of service, support, and quality of technology. It put AOL, not its detractors, in charge of its own destiny.

- *They ride their way through trouble in a nonreactive way.* They have to do this because of the sheer pace of change—"Internet years" meaning a few months of clock time—plus the volatility and uncertainty of everything about Internet business, technology, investor confidence, and competition. If they try to adjust their strategies to meet short-term demands, they lose their business model advantage. The market is paying for Price/Vision, not Price/Earnings. If the vision becomes unclear or loses credibility, the earnings aren't there anyway and efforts to juggle with earnings lose the vision. It's a very fine tightrope to walk along, with a very steep drop.

- *They are very well-managed* and crystal clear about their business model. They have strong executive teams in place in the areas most critical to the business model. Generally, the initial strengths are in marketing and technology; as the firm grows, operations and finance take on an increasing importance. In other words, they build a power brand, not just a Web site.

The last point is critical. While baby gorillas can grow through the enthusiasm and energy of an entrepreneurial team, whatever its age or background, all the gorillas are superbly managed. If they weren't, whatever .com edge they had would soon disappear.

THE MANAGEMENT AGENDA: POWER BRANDS FOR SUCCESS OR SURVIVAL

Most companies will never be a power brand nor will they even try to be one. They won't be spending half a billion dollars or more on marketing or acquiring company after company. If that's the case, why should they pay more than cursory attention to the high-risk, high-hype Internet brand game? The two main reasons to do so boil down to this: success and survival.

All companies have to take into account the main implications of the power brand business model: there are no industry boundaries any more. Wal-Mart changed the rules for main street merchants, suppliers, and established retailers like Kmart as it expanded into new locations. Web players can expand into any location—Schwab, Ameritrade, Amazon, AutoByTel, and others have gone global without having to do much more than set up a marketing program and sign up allies in individual countries. They can become banks, distributors, intermediaries, and retailers through APIs.

If Amazon decides to be an online bank, it's an online bank. Going back to Craigg Ballance's power of e view of the Internet world, if a firm is just an e^1 company, it's limited by its industry and at the same time vulnerable to an e^4 superplayer. Every company that plans to be around as the Internet future unfolds has to take the power brands into account in its own business model. Even the decision to ignore them should be a real decision and not one made by default.

For example, when banks consider their likely future competition, they generally think mainly of the obvious competitors, such as Citibank and Bank of America. They may consider the new online banks, such as Wingspan and Telebanc, or traditional banks that are making heavy investments in Internet capabilities and services, such as Wells Fargo or Citibank with its Citi f/i. But any power brand is a likely competitor, because it has drawing power and, more important, it has by definition built a relationship of trust with its customer base. People trust Amazon and Yahoo more than they may trust their insurance company or any new .com.

Which Internet power brands of today are likely to add full-service banking or insurance to their offers? How will they do so? Obvious candidates are Schwab, Yahoo, and E*Trade, whose ambitions are to be full-service, lifetime relationship portals. E*Trade acquired Telebanc in 1999. Yahoo can be in the banking business in a matter of months via APIs and collaborative agreements. Either as a part or full owner of an online bank or in its role as a portal, it may charge fees to a selected number of banks for them to benefit from its over 100 million subscriber base. Or it may work out a deal with a single bank to co-market or co-brand financial services. There are also less obvious candidates and even unknowns.

And watch out for Wal-Mart. It bought a bank in mid-1999, a move that was later blocked by regulators. Could this be part of its as-yet-unannounced business model for exploiting and extending its own power brand as the preeminent retailer? It has 100 million customers, of whom around 15 percent do not have bank accounts. Hence they don't have credit cards and hence they aren't Internet shoppers. A very plausible scenario is shown in Box 8.1.

The Wal-Mart scenario is not meant as a prediction but as an example of the extent to which an online power brand can easily extend its offers and intrude on an industry through its relationship strengths. Will Amazon become a bank? Why not?

There's no compelling answer to that "why not?" Thus the obvious question for all banks is, What do we offer to the customer relationship that differentiates us from an Internet power brand? The standard answer

Box 8.1. Wal-Mart in Cyberspace

Wal-Mart builds on its 1999 base. It has made a large deal with AOL whereby AOL gets a physical presence in Wal-Mart's stores and Wal-Mart gets a presence on AOL's massive online mall, where 20 million customers park daily.

Wal-Mart/AOL provides low-cost Internet access to the many rural areas of the country that today get poor service from ISPs.

It signs up customers to its bank, offering them perhaps an option of a debit card equivalent for online shopping rather than a credit card; the purchase payment is debited to their checking account when the goods are ordered.

It adds new banking services relevant to its retailing, including perhaps loans for large items such as stereo systems or home office computers and peripherals.

Customers order online and pick up the goods at their nearest Wal-Mart store, sparing Wal-Mart the need to apply the 11 percent shipping charge that consumers increasingly see as the semi-hidden extra that more than offsets the low prices of many Internet retailers.

may involve proven expertise in service and processing, scale, security, capital strengths, and local presence. Those aren't very convincing responses. They take us to the second reason for all companies to consider the implications of the power brand business model template. If you're not going to be a hub that draws customers in, you have to be a spoke in a network complex where you're accessed from a portal or hub—such as a power brand.

Given how easy it is in the age of the Internet for power brands to intrude and weaken the branding and relationship power of many product companies, every company must be actively conscious of brand and its impact. If you're not going to be a brand, you're going to be just a site. If you're not a power player, you're a reactor. In any case, with the accelerated pace of change, you'd better find a business model soon. Do as the brand builders do:

- Determine whether becoming—or even striving to become—a power brand is right for your company.
- Take power brands into account, whether your company strives to be one or not.
- Be well managed and ride out trouble in a nonreactive way.
- Build a powerful brand that you can use in any way that makes sense.
- Market, market, market.

And, perhaps most important, ask yourself: What is your firm's brand in the Internet economy? In answering, remember that a brand is a promise, an identity, and a trust relationship. Above all, recognize that the Internet means the death of traditional product brand equity. E-services—the accelerating shift to electronic agents and brokers—will be the nails in the coffin. As Toys "R" Us shows, a strong offline brand can transfer well to the Web because amid all the ever-growing numbers of Web sites, many people will simplify their search by looking for a familiar and trusted name. But that's the only brand name advantage. After that, the company has to earn its online branding edge.

9

TRANSFORM YOUR CAPITAL AND COST STRUCTURES

Where is the profit on the Internet? At .profit, it's everywhere; until then—and even then—it's hidden between the lines.

Every business revolution has been built on massive capital deployment—the imperial expansion of Europe, the Industrial Revolution, and mass production, to name obvious instances. Massive capital deployment also transformed the economics of business in terms of cost structures, margins, and capital efficiency. The Internet is following the very same pattern, with the same uncertainties, risks, and long gaps between putting capital in and taking profits out. Is it a revolution? Who will succeed?

The current conventional wisdom is that very few Internet players will ever be profitable. That may well be true—but don't discount the fact that the ones that do reach .profit will be very, very profitable. That's an easy prediction to make because we're already seeing plenty of instances. But you have to define *profitable* in the way that entrepreneurs and savvy investors do: cash flow and cost of capital. Accounting conventions distort the dynamics of capital and cost structures in the very same way that individuals distort personal reports of their profits to the IRS. Taxpayers don't try to maximize reported gross income and after-tax profits; they take all the deductions they reasonably can and are delighted to find ones that reduce taxes. In a similar way, the Internet is very profitable, even for some companies that are reporting earnings losses.

As discussed in Chapter Three, if marketing expenses and R&D were capitalized as investments in the future instead of expenses for the present, a lot of Internet companies would suddenly turn profitable—and start paying taxes. If this occurred, many of them would then slip back rather than move ahead on the .profit path. A company must establish itself as a relationship firm that creates value to its customers. If it can't, it won't get through the breakeven point where it can exploit the economic opportunity of the Internet. That makes transformation of capital and cost structures even more critical as a value imperative: the combination of perfect relationships, logistics, and power branding is already creating firms that are, by any of today's standards, value machines both for customers and for themselves.

The business goal here is:

Acknowledge the Internet's capital revolution and move toward negative working capital. Minimize the invested balance sheet capital deployed to support revenue growth, and increase incremental operating margins. Show a path to .profit that establishes a Price/Vision premium in investors' valuation of the company's future, so that you can obtain the investment capital needed to be a major player in the upcoming Internet eras.

Because Internet business is so new, and because—to put it mildly—the start-ups have such unusual financial statements, it's been hard to make sense of the economics of life on the Internet. The .com mentality made revenue growth the target—build traffic and sales. IPO fever and Internet hype talked as if economics were irrelevant. And generally accepted accounting principles obscured the cash and capital dynamics of Internet business. Those dynamics are becoming more and more clear. The blueprint for the business model of today's successful Price/Vision winners is a blueprint for transforming capital structures and cost structures.

There are three general economic business models that companies are following in this new competitive era:

- In the *standard earnings business model,* success is measured by the figures on the Profit and Loss statement and measures of return on capital.

- The *revenue growth business model* has been the dominant if often implicit model behind most .com efforts. It works on the assumption that the driver of growth is market share. Build that and then fine-tune the business machine by exploiting learning curves, improving quality, and using scale and volume to reduce average costs.
- The *capital and margin transformation business model* is the .profit model. It's expensive: it demands heavy initial investment, most of which is treated under accounting rules as an expense to be charged directly against revenues, dragging profits down. It's difficult to implement: at the same time as the company is pushing hard and fast to build a strong customer base, it must be very disciplined in ensuring the operating margin base that will be the key to long-term profitability. That demands immense process competence.

The difference between the transformation model and the standard earnings model is capital. In the standard earnings model, capital is an asset and is shown on the balance sheet as such—working capital, including receivables and inventories, plus fixed assets. The bet that the transformers are making is that they can leverage their revenues through electronic services to generate far more money on far less invested capital than standard earnings players. This literally turns the balance sheet around, turning assets into liabilities. For instance, Dell and Amazon each collect their money immediately from consumers (and quickly from businesses) but pay their suppliers more than thirty days later. In the standard model, the firm should have a positive working capital to be seen as efficient and in sound financial health. In the transformation model, this is turned upside down. .Profit firms often have the advantage of *negative* working capital; they do not tie up capital that has a high carrying cost. This is part of the reason that Amazon is cash flow positive even when it's reporting large losses.

THE CAPITAL ACQUISITION CHALLENGE

There are two categories of capital: *investor input capital*, which gives the firm money to spend, and *balance sheet capital*, which is money spent on working capital and fixed assets. The transformation player initially needs plenty of investor input capital for marketing and for building technology infrastructures. To move from simple .com Web sites to implementing the value imperatives, companies must also spend an often unanticipated extra amount of money *because* of their success—on ensuring scalability in the technology base, customer support and service, order fulfillment, and so on. As it grew bigger and faster, for instance, Amazon had to move into the warehousing business and is spending an estimated $300 million to build supercenters. That will increase its invested capital—and that capital cost must be offset by increased operating margins.

Capital must be obtained from somewhere, most obviously from venture capitalists and through Initial Public Offerings (IPOs). It's here that the issue of Price/Vision comes right to the forefront. Without capital, you can't get into the transformation game for two obvious reasons: you need to move very fast and very aggressively and spend money well in advance of the operating profits to support all the costs. That means you have to convince investors you have some chance of a very big win indeed.

The company that can pull in the capital to fund the first run along the path and keep the stock price high transforms the rules of capital deployment. It pays less and less for more and more when it seeks to acquire another firm. This is fundamental to the transformation template—in a way, investors aren't so much buying your stock as authorizing you to acquire any company you need, using their equity in your company as the currency of exchange. So the transformers pay in stock, essentially transferring a claim on part of their future value. All others pay in cash.

In getting on the Internet, most of the expenditures center on the Web site technology base and the cost of handling transactions; these can be just a few thousand dollars. But marketing is another story: The average first-year marketing cost to get business on a portal is $5 million.[1] Obviously, a firm can't play in the transformation game without plenty of capital—not thousands, but many millions. A few examples of the scale of the money needed to fund major Internet business platform initiatives:

- Schwab's executive vice president for advertising, a veteran of the long-distance advertising wars of the 1980s, estimates that it costs around $300 million, "sustained for many years, to build and maintain a brand as a household name."[2]

- The Boston Consulting Group states that the typical "cyberretailer" spends 65 percent of its revenues on marketing and advertising, versus 5 percent for a brick-and-mortar merchant.[3]
- According to the Gartner Group, a "transaction-enabled" Web site costs $1.5 to $3 million to set up. For financial services, the figure is closer to $15 million. A Forrester survey of fifty companies found that 30 percent spent between $500,000 and $5 million.[4]

In 1969, the leader of the U.S. Senate said, "A billion here, a billion there. Pretty soon, it runs into real money." Updated, this is, "A billion here, a billion there, and pretty soon that's the Internet economy." Senator Dirksen was speaking of spending money raised by taxes and deficit borrowing—over three decades ago. Business today is going to have to spend massive sums of money—a billion here and a billion there—to build and keep its customer base; to design, implement, operate, and extend technology infrastructures; and to provide customer support. It needs new capital to do this.

According to the *New York Times,* the top ten online brokers alone budgeted $1.5 billion for their own advertising in the year 2000.[5] They had to. Marketing is the single largest and most urgent investment for most Internet players, larger even than their technology investments. Ameritrade, one of the online services that transformed the entire landscape of securities trading, illustrates this need. It made a profit on its operations: $15 million on revenues of $186 million in 1998. It announced that it will spend $200 million on marketing in eighteen months through the end of 2000, compared with $65 million for the preceding eighteen months, as well as $150 million to upgrade its network. In September 1999, Ameritrade warned analysts that its customer acquisition costs have risen to $500. Its growth rests on the effectiveness—and scale—of its marketing.

As we've noted, this marketing is technically an expense and not capital in terms of how it's handled on financial statements. Marketing costs are deducted as they are incurred. But for most Internet growth businesses, they're capital in two ways:

- First, they are an investment made ahead of the market; that is you either have to spend all this money when you don't have the earnings to cover it so as to build the business base, or you have to pay for your marketing out of existing resources and drain today's earnings. That makes marketing more like R&D.

- Second, because you don't have the earnings to cover your marketing costs, you have to attract long-term investment capital to pay for them. So, even though they don't appear on the balance sheet as capital, they really are.

What Internet business thus involves is a capital shift, most obviously from physical capital—the stuff that does show up on the balance sheet—to what is loosely termed *intellectual capital,* which doesn't. Marketing costs are an investment in customer relationship capital.

ECONOMIC VALUE ADDED VERSUS EARNINGS

Capital and innovation go together. Capital funds the future. It's obtained in the past, owned in the present, and deployed to generate innovation for the future. It has a carrying cost: the direct after-tax cost of debt plus the more implicit cost of equity capital, which is harder to calculate. Economic profit—as opposed to paper earnings—is the real "free" cash flow generated by operations, less the cost of the capital used to create it.

There are several different terms for this profit equation, which focuses not on the bottom line as reported on income statements but on the efficient use of capital to generate the earnings. The most widely adopted term is economic value added (EVA), a trademark of Stern, Stewart. While there are challenges to the details of the approach, the arguments underlying the formal calculations of EVA are indisputable.[6]

Standard accounting measures of profitability ignore the cost of the capital used by the firm to generate its after-tax cash flow. Allocations, depreciation, methods of valuing inventory, and the like distort the cash flow picture and ignore the cost of equity. In effect, if two firms have basically the same earnings and balance sheet position today but one has a higher market valuation, its cost of capital is lower than that of the other firm.

There is no correlation over the longer term between market value and any standard accounting measure of profitability, such as earnings per share, return on assets, return on investment, and the like. There is, however, a consistent relationship between economic value added and market value added. That is, the market clearly bids prices up or down on the basis of the efficient use of financial capital to generate free cash flow. The market is paying for value now, not earnings now. It's looking at the value path, not the earnings picture. Obviously, there are many distortions in this general picture: speculators, managers of funds who face pressure to generate returns this quarter, and day traders who ignore the financial structures of the firm whose stock they buy. That said, MVA and EVA move together.

EVA and related terms that vary mainly in technical details (and consulting firms' claim to conceptual and methodological superiority) started to displace traditional measures of return on investment and earnings growth in corporate finance and strategic planning around the same time as the Web appeared. That was coincidental. EVA has nothing to do with the Internet but the Internet does have everything to do with EVA. We are not so concerned here with the financial and technical details of EVA as with its well-established messages about generating real profitability versus reporting profits. EVA applies to the world of the Internet just as much as any other period of business and any other area of business. Indeed, it explains much of what commentators see as bizarre about valuations of Internet stocks and Internet players' stream of losses.

We see two main EVA implications for Internet business:

• Value rests on a combination of cash flow generation and capital leverage, not so much for today but for the medium-term future—two to five years. This is why it's not at all unrealistic for a company to be very highly valued and become even more so as its reported losses grow. Conversely, its price could fall as profits grow.

• The market is looking for *value* now. That value may come from earnings now and in the very near future, as it does for most established companies. But just as Intel, for example, could more than double its earnings immediately just by halving its R&D, a baby gorilla could often become profitable *now* just by cutting its marketing (that's certainly the case for Amazon) and slowing down its infrastructure investments. If Intel announced it was slashing R&D, its stock price would plummet. In doing so, it would increase its earnings but reduce its value.

The point is worth repeating: Accounting conventions and tax laws handle capital in ways that may not accurately capture the dynamics of Internet business. From a business perspective, there are some obvious absurdities in many of today's "generally accepted accounting principles," the mantra of the accounting profession. If a firm invests in R&D, that's handled as an expense and reduces reported pretax earnings because it's deducted as a cost in the year it's spent. Buy a building for the same amount and that's capitalized on the balance sheet. It's depreciated over many years, leading to a lower tax deduction for this year. The cash flow expenditure may be the same in both cases, but the EVA impact is very different. Ironically, the lower deduction often reduces EVA because the net cash flow of the company is *improved* by reducing the earnings. The larger deduction for the R&D versus the building purchase cuts taxes. Invest in buildings and you look more profitable. Spend the very same amount of money on marketing and you make less profit, which means you generate *more* cash flow, because you pay less tax. So a bricks-and-mortar bookstore has an accounting edge over an online one. Does it have a value edge, though?

The old industrial model was based on earnings, not cash flow. Financial accounting overlooked the cost of capital. It also used a lot of working capital—raw materials, work in process, finished goods inventory, accounts receivable, and so on—with a lot of long-term capital tied up in fixed assets—buildings and equipment, for example. Well before the emergence of the Internet as a business resource, EVA highlighted the fact that a key element in generating economic profits is to minimize the capital used to produce a given level of cash flow from operations.

Obviously, this is the very core of much of logistics, online relationships, electronic out-tasking, branded hub collaborations, and many other components of the business model templates we describe in *From .com to .profit*. In this regard, .profit business is EVA in action. Many gorillas and baby gorillas are showing a value path that rests on using less overall capital to generate more business than other companies in which individuals and institutions could choose to invest. They will readily accept negative accounting earnings as long as they perceive that a high EVA structure is at the end of the path.

The details of EVA are extremely complex and expert investors spend much of their time and skill looking for indicators of value and operational indicators that may change their assessment of a firm. Executives and advisers spend just as much on tax issues—the best source of cash flow for many "unprofitable" firms, just as it is for owners of sports teams. (Let's not forget that no one buys a football team to make an earnings profit. It's primarily a way of generating reported financial statement losses via depreciation of players' long-term contracts. Yet after years of "losses," the team is sold for a massive capital gain, because the cash flows from the losses are so substantial.)

The metrics of particular relevance to investors and executives are those that are indicators of progress and roadblocks along the value path. For example, in late 1999, as the growth in new customers slowed among leading online securities trading companies, acquisition cost per customer was being carefully watched.

OBTAINING CAPITAL—AT HYPERSPEED

Capital has to be invested today to be competitive tomorrow. And it has to be invested in massive amounts today, with "tomorrow" looking a long way off when we're talking about economic payoff, but dangerously near when we're looking at business model priorities and at competitors already ahead in their business model implementation.

Where's the typical firm going to get the capital? How will it pay for it? Who will share the value it produces and the risks it generates? The old answer was that it would come from risk capital. The explosive growth of Web commerce and related infrastructures and services has been funded almost entirely by venture capitalists providing start-up investments, individuals and institutions buying into IPOs, and both speculators and long-term investors bidding up the value of Internet players' market capitalization.

Certainly, that model has produced massive innovation and created massive wealth. Its effectiveness can be seen by comparing the U.S. experience with that of Europe. By the end of 1999, there were already more than a dozen firms in the United States that were each selling over a billion dollars of goods and services a year over the Net. There was not a single one in Europe or Asia; there isn't an equivalent of Dell, Amazon, or eBay because a pool of venture capital developed only recently.

Venture capital is expensive. To get it, you have to give away part of your company forever. Obviously, the more that investors see and believe , in your value path, the more they bid up the value of your stock, which reduces your cost of capital. The gorillas like Cisco and baby gorillas like eToys have an edge over other companies by the very fact that their cost of capital is so much lower than their competitors'. They can make acquisitions for less real money than the others because they have convinced the market of their value path. They have generated a Price/Vision premium through their business model.

Red Herring aptly summarizes the link between successful business models and the cost of capital for the firms that own them: "The biggest benefit of being a gorilla in your category is the ability to access low-cost capital either through private investment or the public markets. This position also provides Web entrepreneurs with high market capitalizations that they can leverage to acquire new services, along with privileged partnership opportunities that can expand their audience reach."[7]

That simple statement summarizes the reality of .profit: the Internet is as much a capital revolution as a technological one. It's a revolution in the scale of capital, the principles on which it is obtained, how it is deployed, and what its payoffs are. The very idea of negative working capital as a virtue and of massive losses as the basic reason for valuing a company far more highly than its competitors would have been viewed even five years ago as at least eccentric and more probably as downright stupid. You won't find it in any mainstream textbooks on corporate finance; they were written a few years ago.

Those few years are what the revolution is really about—urgency. The pace of change in every area of the .profit drive—business, technology, customer response, electronic globalization, and business model impact—is so great that massive capital has to be obtained and deployed very quickly. Companies are using that capital for revenue and customer growth now— to create profits later. Obviously, at some stage they will have to reduce their rate of investment and start rewarding their investors with a flow of tangible value. The winners will be able to do so because they will have the value base—a combination of perfect logistics, perfect relationships, channel harmony, transformed capital and cost structures, power brands, and established intermediary positions. These will then be the players of the next phase: not e-business, e-commerce, or even e-services—but simply business (with the e assumed). But they don't have time to spare.

The .com era came in and is going out in just four to five years. When it began, many companies decided to stay out of the game; it was too risky, too expensive, and too unstable. Those that now don't want to stand still and watch their current business model strengths erode to the degree that they will be sideline watchers as electronic commerce turns into plain commerce have two choices:

1. *Minimize capital commitments.* Stay within the .com boundaries and basically just set up a transaction Web site—probably hosted by one of the many firms that specialize in this growing area—and you can limit expenditures. You can pay a fee to one of the power brand consumer portals or to a business-to-business hub. At best, this option is defensive reaction. For a small company, it means marginalization. For a large one, it means risking a fractured business model.

2. *Find the money somehow.* The immediate question is, Where do you find the money? Then ask, Why should anyone give you the capital and what will they get in return? For a company that already has the money because it has the earnings to carry the investment, the second question shifts to, What impact does this have on what your current investors are getting? The answers in all cases come back to the business model. If you are valued on an as-is Price/Earnings basis, then investors have very little if any reason to give you capital; they are very likely to bid an established company's stock down and not up as it begins any large investments that don't point to value and then to .profit. And they are increasingly unlikely to grab at a new firm's stock just because it's an Internet IPO: the glow around .com start-ups is fading fast and will fade faster as investors back off from the very high valuations of Internet stocks.

MODELING FOR PRICE/VISION

A new firm has to bring something special to get the Price/Vision ratio that finding the money demands. It has to be a baby gorilla. Ariba is an example—its business model is superb and there can be little question that it will grow and plenty of reason to believe it will be very profitable. Its Operations Resource Management System software dramatically reduces the cost, complexity, and staffing involved in procurement of the operating resources that consume around a third of a company's cost base: equipment purchases, office supplies, professional services, and the like. All these savings go straight to the bottom line.

In its first two years of operation, Ariba's revenues grew from $630 thousand in fiscal 1997 to $6.2 million in 1998, with over $20 million estimated for 1999. But its sales and marketing expenses remain larger than its revenues; they fuel the growth. Its accumulated R&D costs for software amounted to over $11 million between its inception in September 1996 and March 1999—around $1.5 million a quarter. Add to that the hardware and network equipment and facilities that comprise most of the $4 million of long-term assets on Ariba's balance sheet and it's obvious that there was no way Ariba could fund its growth by itself.

In its early years, it relied on venture capital, the traditional source. Before it launched its very successful IPO in June 1999, around 30 percent of its equity was owned by the venture capital groups and individual investors that provided Ariba with much of its $20 million in operating capital. Without this risk capital, Ariba would not have been positioned for any IPO. Its market capitalization the very first day of trading was $4 billion: there is plenty of wealth creation to share between Ariba founders and employees, venture capital providers, and institutional investors.

How many companies have a business model as compelling as Ariba's? How many companies have any chance whatsoever of attracting such investors as it has? What do you do if you have just a pretty good business model? Then it's a little like being a center for an average NBA team. You're one of the top two hundred players in the world but Tim Duncan and Shaquille O'Neal are going to dunk you. You're in the same league and you're in the same game, but you don't quite have the tools.

We've mentioned the concept of increasing returns—to those that have, more is given. A gorilla has a competitive edge and a market valuation edge. A baby gorilla also has an edge in very much the same way. It gets funded at a level that in and of itself gives it an immediate advantage over other players. A medium-size software company can't match Ariba in pace or scale of growth. It will go broke before it reaches breakeven. Ariba's breakeven requirement is postponed by its investor capital.

For companies in retailing, banking, manufacturing, and distribution, the picture is the same. There will be few baby gorillas and even fewer gorillas, but however small their number and their market share, they are a threat to all other players. Not only can they fracture the latters' business models, they can fracture their capital models, too. This means that every firm in an ecosystem with well-funded baby gorillas simply must find a way to build its own Price/Vision premium. There are three main ways of doing this:

- Develop a business model edge and seek out risk investors.
- Set up a separate company that will be valued on a different basis from the parent and seek out risk investors.
- Position the company to be acquired.

One way or another, every firm has to get out of the trap of increasing returns to its rivals and keeping a Price/Earnings straitjacket for itself.

Develop a Business Model Edge

If a company does not have a clearly articulated business model and communicate it convincingly, then it's out of the .profit innovation game and at best confined to an evolutionary .com approach. The value imperatives that we present can be adapted by any company. But it has to move fast, inventory its strengths, and—in most instances—substitute relationships, collaboration, and community for financial capital.

The imperative for perfecting logistics is an obvious priority. Move quickly to produce a substantial reduction in working capital and overhead. If there's an appropriate intermediary hub that can help you improve your own logistics, sign up on it very fast. That's the pull of Ariba, Chemdex, VerticalNet, and other vortals: they are already in place (generally well funded from risk capital) and they provide a fast logistics payoff. Similarly, Application Service Providers (ASPs) provide fast access to software without the need to commit to heavy fixed costs for development or purchase of packages. Businesses everywhere are reshaping by slashing overhead. The results show up very quickly on a firm's income statement and differentiate it from its competitors equally quickly. Doing so will increase your market valuation and thus cut your cost of capital. You will be able to deploy the economic value added it creates to start funding your .profit future.

Look to collaborate where you can. Don't think of your .com Web site as an island. Exploit opportunities for channel harmonization. View your entire distribution chain as a win-win target of opportunity. Seek out communities such as trade associations. Partnerships needn't be formal joint ventures and may be the cheapest form of capital. The wonders of application program interfaces (APIs) allow you to build electronic partnerships with UPS or Federal Express, banks, and other companies that complement, extend, or support your own offers and operations. Take advantage of the savings these can offer.

Set Up a Separate Company

One approach to both the business and financial challenges of Internet business is to set up a new company. Banc One, for instance, created Wingspan in mid-1999. Its advertising was pretty specific about its reasoning, which seems to be a majority view among commentators on Internet business: start from scratch with an organization that is not constrained by anything—whether structure, traditions, procedures, incentives and rewards, staff and management profiles, or dress code. Wingspan defines itself as a bank designed to innovate and one that is not built from the bureaucracy downward.

The major economic advantage of a separate company is that it can be valued separately and has the opportunity to attract venture capital. It's freer to establish its own alliances, too. Many firms now set up subsidiaries that provide what is termed a "tracking stock," providing a base for the market to place a value on the Internet business component of the enterprise and helping attract top talent. There has always been a shortage of skills and experience in the information technology field—around one in ten jobs advertised goes unfilled—but the Internet expansion makes the problem far more difficult. The variety of new technologies and their pace of change plus the complexity of development, integration, and operation mean that the best talent can command more than just a premium. It's close to impossible for most firms to attract even junior specialists without offering them stock options. In the race to .com, business management was an afterthought for many start-ups (if it was even a thought), but it's a priority for .profit players. As a result, they are seeking to lure away successful executives from Fortune 1000 firms. Here again, companies have to offer an attractive package that includes a share of the growth in value that recruits help generate.

There are thus many arguments in favor of spinning off the firm's Internet business into a separate organization. They all relate to growth and urgency. There are counterarguments, though, that relate to coordination and integration. A challenge in setting up such new ventures is determining just how independent they will be from the parent. In the case of Wingspan, it's effectively a competitor of Banc One, and its ads are implicitly a criticism of its founder and patron. The new is a rival to the old, not a complement to it. Other risks include multiple and conflicting processes, no clear organizational identity, and limited channel harmony—if any. Wingspan's likelihood of success is uncertain.

Whether to build a .com capability from within or to build it on the outside will be one of the key questions for managers in many firms over the next few years. The experience at Schwab shows that the in-house option can work superbly. Schwab blends the strengths of offline and online. Among the business-to-business logistics leaders, many companies have done the same.

Position the Company to Be Acquired

If you want to be acquired, build sufficient intellectual capital to be of value to another firm that has plenty of access to investment capital. This represents a major shift in business thinking. Prior to the surge of .com start-ups, founders of new companies generally looked to build them up. That's been replaced in many entrepreneurs' thinking by the goal of growing fast and selling soon. The gorillas are in a hurry and they look for small companies that fill a gap in their capabilities, provide new technology and skills, and open up opportunities to innovate. Baby gorillas often explicitly aim at being acquired by a gorilla, with stock options a lure.

The very nature of .profit business makes it certain that the pace of acquisition will increase. Collaboration demands extension of technology capabilities, ability to include new services and partners within the firm's offers. Often, these will be handled through partnerships, portal fees, commissions, and other contracting. But in many instances, it will make plenty of sense for a strong player with Price/Vision market valuation to spare to buy a much smaller firm when doing so will in itself increase its own perceived .profit opportunity. Of course, there are plenty of firms jostling to be acquired for the very same reason.

Do Something: Pick an Option

The three options we've described can each attract capital to fund the future and lower its cost. The business model edge shifts the focus of investor valuation, reducing cost of capital for an existing firm and attracting a better offer from venture capital firms for a new one. The very purpose of setting up a separate company is largely to maximize opportunities to leverage Price/Vision and be able to obtain capital on better terms than as part of its parent. Positioning to be acquired looks to establish a value premium just by being there.

There are plenty of examples of successes and failures in each of these three areas. They all relate to EVA. EVA relates to .profit. .Profit relates to the business model. And the business model relates to capital and cost of capital. They each require the firm to compete for capital in a complex and volatile market. In almost all instances, the deal will involve giving away a share of—or all of—the company in return for venture money, a successful IPO, or an acquisition.

This capital literally buys time for the firm. But it will run out of time if it can't generate an economic payback from the capital. That won't happen if it has the economic structures of the traditional firm. It must change its own capital and cost structures to generate long-term EVA on its capital from its investors.

THE MANAGEMENT AGENDA: CAPITAL, COST, AND OVERHEAD

Overhead is what is left over after all the waste is taken out. And waste has to be taken out, simply because the leaders in using the Internet to transform their cost structures got that way by doing so. We cited examples in our chapters on perfecting logistics and perfecting long-term relationships. Customer self-management in particular cuts administrative and support costs.

The heavy burden of marketing expenses distorts the fact that Internet business transforms operating margins. The "bricks" company that is profitable on paper risks being slaughtered in the coming years by "clicks" that now are loss-makers on their financial statements. Digital products have extremely high margins and low costs for people, inventory, and physical assets. It may take a decade before we see which companies do manage to stabilize and then reduce their marketing costs. The companies that successfully make use of the marketing investment, innovate through capital they've obtained, and generate earnings through economic value added are the companies that will then build a substantial Price/Vision premium, whether through business model edge, setting up a separate company, or positioning to be acquired. These are the companies that will benefit from their capital and cost structure advantage. This advantage, above all, is the business transformation the Internet is generating.

The .com era basically ignored finance, with a combination of excuses:

- The Web was a low-cost new channel.
- Hits would build revenue base and revenues mean profits.
- You can't afford not to be a player in the online game.

These are now unacceptable excuses. The economics of online business must be placed at the very top of the management agenda. Each of the value imperatives in itself affects cost and margin transformation—positively and negatively. Table 9.1 sets forth a checklist to help guide the agenda.

And what of all these changes? What will they mean for your company? How will you complete the final column of our checklist? Are you ready for the revolution that's hidden there?

The word *revolution* is too often and too easily thrown around. Real revolutions are brutal and messy. Quite often the revolutionary leaders are overtaken by events—that is, they get executed. At the end of the revolution, there's a move back to the old days in a new form. So, in the French Revolution, the result was a new emperor, Napoleon, with all his dukes and princes, followed by the restoration of the Bourbon monarchy. The Jacobins found themselves loaded into the tumbrels in their turn, following the aristos they'd dispatched to the guillotine. The "Socialist" regime of

Table 9.1. Imperatives and the Management Agenda

Imperative	Positive Impacts	Negative Impacts	Where are we and what are we going to do?
Perfect your logistics	Massive reduction of working capital per unit of sale. Massive reduction of SGA.	Cost of integration of the technology platform and process base.	??
Cultivate your long-term customer relationships	High digital margins on repeat business. Cost savings from customer self-management.	Cost of marketing and technology infrastructure and customer support.	??
Harmonize your channels on the customer's behalf	Leveraging logistics savings and relationship revenues.	Cost of duplicate channel support.	??
Build a power brand for your business	Revenues from referral fees and commissions at a hub that "spokes" pay to be part of. Low-cost cross-selling.	Massive capital investment on marketing and technology to be sustained for years.	??
Transform your capital and cost structures	Dramatic long-term improvements in cash flow generation, capital efficiency, and ability to benefit from high-margin digital goods and services.	High and fast up-front investments with substantial business and financial risk; stock price volatility; "bet the business" gamble.	??
Become—or use—a value-adding intermediary	High digital margins on low transaction fees.	Start-up costs and capital demands.	??

the Soviet Union looked more and more like that of the Czars—but, of course, Nicholas II had been executed and Trotsky first exiled and then assassinated.

Is the Internet a revolution in capital to match that of the Industrial Revolution? Will many of the revolutionaries—Amazon, eBay, Priceline—die? Will the old guard come back in a new form with AOL/Time Warner as the emperor? Or will it be Wal-Mart the Second?

All we know that is true for all revolutions is that most of the old landowning aristocracy loses and loses forever. So is the Internet a revolution? Count on it.

10

BECOME A VALUE-ADDING INTERMEDIARY—OR USE ONE

The Internet is Paradise—if your company can create value as,
or through, an intermediary.

When the Internet first took off, it was mainly described in terms of information. Remember the Information Superhighway, the Information Age? Those terms sound almost quaint—relics of a distant past. That sort of hype has largely disappeared, but information is still one of the main sources of competitive opportunity. A new opportunity comes from the information distortions that are the norm in business. Customers and suppliers can't easily locate each other so they interact through brokers and agents, who charge a premium fee for their service. The more fragmented the information flow, the more value new intermediaries can offer—and the more they can charge and control.

Car dealers, insurance agents, mortgage brokers, travel agents, and investment advisers won't necessarily be displaced by the flood of new Internet intermediaries that provide the information needed for buyers to get the best deal, for suppliers to bring deals to customers, and for supply chain partners to optimize the entire relationship chain. They won't *necessarily* be displaced—but they probably will be.

Internet business is driven by relationships, collaboration, and community—and fueled by intermediaries that add value to the customer and to the supplier by combining all these. More and more of those intermediaries are Web addresses—thriving Web addresses. The technology base of e-services adds and intensifies the demand for electronic agents, brokers, dynamic offers assembled on the fly, and searches for deals expands with and contributes to ever-increasing personalization and customization. If you're a car dealer or insurance agent, for instance, you'd better match this value. If you're a business looking for the best agent to handle your search for goods, request for bids, offer to sell, or standard supply chain management, it's more and more likely that the very best value provider is a Web trading hub. If you want to buy a car, you can get access to better information than even the dealer has about anything to do with the car you're looking for. And the Internet intermediary will display it with a flourish.

Every firm that is looking to be a Web player needs to seek out value-adding intermediary niches. There are many opportunities and by the very fact that they are value-adding, they provide a fast start to .profit. That makes this the business goal for the value-adding intermediary:

Establish an Internet presence that creates new value for buyers and sellers in their transactions with each other through a combination of information, recommendations, coordination, collaboration, and brokering. Reduce costs and fragmentation in the buyer-seller relationship chain.

And this is the business goal for those companies that choose instead to use value-adding intermediaries rather than join them:

Adapt to the new value-added intermediaries in your field by using them to add value to your own services by reducing costs and fragmentation in the buyer-seller relationship chain.

The Internet, particularly the .com phase of the Internet, has always been about intermediation—disintermediation of middlemen through direct selling and self-service and reintermediation through providing some special value as an electronic middleman. In either case, there's a portal or a hub competing to be a winner in the .profit game, which is about aggregation. Most of the value imperative templates that we have described so far aim at disintermediating some other service provider—that's a polite word for getting customers to bypass it and come to you so you can take away its business.

The last of the six main business model templates that we see in operation, evolution, and often invention today pushes toward new forms of intermediation: becoming a value-adding middleman, coordination point, or broker. The many companies applying it often target an entire supply chain, distribution system, or manufacturer-consumer relationship chain that is anything but value-adding. The existing intermediaries in that context are value-taking, gaining high commissions because of the fragmentation of communication, lack of coordination, and information gaps between buyer and seller.

In the .com era of Internet business, many companies whose main strength was their established offline brand tried to create new intermediaries via a Web site (see Box 10.1). They aimed at becoming portals, gateways, and hubs: powerful intermediaries in the new marketplace. They largely failed.

Now we are seeing more and more new players take a .profit approach to becoming a value-adding intermediary. They have new technology to draw on and are highly focused in their targeting. The .com misconception was that a strong brand can be transferred online. The hub players know they have to build their intermediation value. They do a few things really well, rather than lots of things so-so. There's thus a difference in branding strategy between the power brands of the business model template we described in Chapter Eight and these brands. The latter are carefully narrow and the former aggressively broad. Of course, if one player ever successfully combines the two . . . someone else will be in a lot of trouble.

WORKING TOWARD WIN-WIN

The collaboration imperative lies behind the rise of industry portals and sites like Ariba.com, Marshall, and Chemdex (built on Ariba's software). These all create and sustain relationships between manufacturers and buyers in a fragmented distribution chain. Ariba.com allows all the parties to customize their sites so that all the bureaucracy, paper, and administrivia of procurement disappear. Marshall describes itself as a "junction box" and uses its relationship base to optimize the industry manufacturer-to-user chain, keeping manufacturers informed about buying patterns and trends

---

Box 10.1. Offline Brands: Attempted Intermediaries

- IBM launched its World Avenue mall in 1996. The goal was to provide a shared online mall, with a strong brand name—IBM—plus a large number of storefronts that would attract shoppers to the mutual advantage of each other. It closed in 1997.
- MCI loudly launched its Marketplace MCI, which included such well-known retailers as Nordstrom, Foot Locker, and Omaha Steaks—and quietly closed it a year later.
- The Home Shopping Network, which had been very successful in selling on cable television, similarly failed to transfer its strengths to the Net. It had too many online stores and provided too little added value to the customer.
- In the business-to-business area, Nets Inc. was a hub that attracted plenty of initial business in 1996: 275,000 buyers from 36,000 companies and 75,000 sellers. It got as terrific a press as Amazon or Yahoo and you'll find many books and articles lauding it as the next big Internet winner. It went out of business in 1998.
- In 1995, Time Warner's Pathfinder site was one of the most popular in the Web in terms of hits. It offered free reading of magazines that would cost $150 a month to subscribe to. It failed to attract advertisers—unlike the $150-a-month printed copies—and was quietly closed down in 1999.

---

so that they can adjust their production. Similarly, buyers are kept alert about likely shortages.

Chemdex (which has recently changed its name to Ventro) is another baby gorilla. It captures the trend toward win-win optimization of the manufacturer-buyer link, at the expense of the established broker and distribution system. Formed in 1997 (as Chemdex) to address the needs of researchers in the life sciences who need to locate specialty chemicals that are very hard to find, Ventro now provides a trading hub for the 300,000 buyers and 1,500 suppliers of these products. Because the products are so specialized, catalogs are often out of date and there's no standard description or easy contact point. Researchers typically spend about five hours a week searching through hundreds of catalog pages to locate, say, six vials of a scarce item. The distributors take a margin of as much as 80 percent of the purchase price. Ventro takes just 5 percent.

Its business model is simple: be a hub that offers a win-win opportunity to buyer and seller. The key here is not the technology per se but its core team of Ph.D. scientists who catalog chemicals for its scientist community of buyers, a very complex activity requiring expert knowledge and judgment. In itself, this adds value to all players; classifying the specialty products so that it is easy for buyers to locate what they need is a very difficult process. And, of course, Ventro adds new e-services, including a partnership to ensure delivery of goods far faster than the old system and, also very much "of course," personal catalogs and a Your Favorites section on the site.

Reorganizing Business

Ventro faces many business problems—having the right business model doesn't mean that the company will execute its plans smoothly and quickly or be able to grow fast enough to recover its investments in marketing and technology infrastructure. But just look at its intermediary value-adding capabilities. Within three months of starting up, it had 130 suppliers, through which over 300,000 products are bought and sold with the online catalogs that are updated daily (versus the once-a-year average for the industry's printed catalogs). Transaction costs have been cut from $100 to $10–$20. Smaller manufacturers get online shelf space. Chemical companies typically spend 20 percent of their revenues on marketing and distribution. Ventro shows that it's practical to get that cost way down by linking them to buyers online. And it makes an operating profit on just a 5 percent commission.

Business 2.0 describes the implications: Ventro "is forcing the biggest suppliers to actually compete for the first time in return for big savings on marketing and distribution costs. . . . Do the math. Cost cuts predict price cuts, which stimulate demand. . . . Trusted intermediaries represent a powerful category for the investment community. Long-term, they will reorganize the economy."[1] The phrasing here is intriguing—not revolutionize, transform, or turbocharge the economy, but just "reorganize."

Here's the power of the value-adding intermediaries. AutoByTel, Ventro, and VerticalNet have reorganized business relationship chains—value chains—and done so whether or not they themselves become profitable. It's rather like Visicalc, the software company that invented the spreadsheet via the Apple II. It died. Apple lost its preeminent position in early personal computers. Lotus 1-2-3 and Excel took over. But Visicalc and Apple had, by then, already reorganized the rules of the game.

The value-adding intermediaries or hubs look like being the Visicalcs of the .profit business era. Some of them will be sure to become the Lotuses and Excels; that is, some of them will make money. The more inefficient and value-draining the transaction chain they focus on, the more certain it is that over time they and others will displace it.

With Ariba.com and Ventro, the portal is community-enabling and community-driven. Genentech, the biotechnology innovator, made it clear even before Ventro was in operation that it expected its own scientists, the university labs it collaborates with, and the manufacturers it buys from to get up on the portal. Similarly, HP and Cisco announced within ten days of Ariba.com going live that each was shifting its supply chain onto it—around $70 billion of procurement a year. Within three months, this figure grew to over $100 billion. It marks a shift from supply chain *management* to supply chain community *coordination*.

Dynamic Brokering

This shift is the inevitable prelude to dynamic brokering, where the software itself adds to the relationship interactions. An early example is Metalsite.com, which brings together the community of large-scale steel manufacturers and buyers to trade excess inventory. Weirton Steel, the main sponsor of the initiative, sells $1.5 billion a year through this new vehicle, a 10 percent revenue increase on the same volume. The Metalsite commission fee is under 2.5 percent. The buyer gets a better purchase price—around 15 percent lower—while the seller gets a higher net price through the elimination of the higher broker fee it used to pay.

There are many varieties of value-adding intermediaries. There are *vertical* hubs—Altra Energy, Band-X (telecommunications), SciQuest (life sciences), Cattle Offerings, e-Steel, Paper Exchange, PlasticNet. The world's first insurance industry portal, ebix.com, is a vertical next-generation portal designed to meet the insurance needs of the consumer and insurance professional. Then there are *functional* hubs such as Processors Unlimited, which handles reverse logistics—the disposal of returned goods—as well as MBO.com, for procurement of services for maintenance and repairs; Employease, for managing employee benefits; and Adauction, which auctions off unused television advertising space.

Most trading hubs don't attract much general attention. That's because they tend to be of most value when they focus on the unique needs, processes, and features of a supply chain community. The hub can then customize its services. An example is Realbid, an online market for institutional buyers and sellers of commercial real estate. The buyers are typically pension funds and insurance companies who get hundreds of sales proposals a week. Most of these contain hundreds of pages of information and frequently get tossed if they come from an unfamiliar source.

Realbid focuses entirely on the initial part of the sale, with a site that strips out anything that does not relate to buyers' finding properties that meet their requirements, as expressed by their answers to five to ten online questions. They will spend perhaps a hundred hours researching a property that interests them. An executive for Realbid summarizes its role as "purposefully limited. . . . But the 2–5 minutes they spend with us eliminates hours." Here, as in so many specialized buyer-seller interactions, users don't want to browse or surf, the attraction offered by more general purpose service providers. Industry-specific knowledge of what information is vital for making a sale strips away "noise" and "hindrance."[2] In a similar fashion, Fresh Commodity Exchange offers a single contact point for finding prices on broccoli, cauliflower, and other vegetables, a process that previously required buyers to make up to thirty phone calls for each item.

Consumer Finance Network (CFN) saves employees of large companies an average of $500 on auto insurance. It markets its services only to human resource departments and offers only price quotes on the best deals from forty-six financial service providers of car, life, and home insurance, mortgage refinancing, and long-term care protection. Five hundred of DaimlerChrysler's staff saved $5 million on insurance, for instance. *Gartner Executive Edge* explains why this is possible. "Because this [insurance] market is so glaringly inefficient, an efficient market maker such as CFN will expose glaring non-competitive pricing issues."[3] State regulation of insurance has resulted in variations in auto insurance of as much as $800 for the same coverage. The article reports that in some states there are as many as twenty thousand permutations on basic policies. The agency system, of course, greatly adds to the price of insurance; in some instances, the commission amounts to two years' premiums. CFN is "price-neutral." It takes the same fee for sale of a policy from all its providers. It gathers customer data, broadcasts it to the providers who respond with offers, and arranges payment, including by credit card.

Together, these examples illustrate the variety and dynamism of the value-adding intermediaries. They raise a serious management issue for every company. What do you do if you're part of the system they're targeting for attack? More generally, what do you do if you face a competitor with just 1 percent market share operating via *any* of these business model templates?

OPPORTUNITIES IN SUPPLY CHAIN COMMUNITIES

At any point in time, a new e-services player may suddenly find a niche to fill. The most useful way for a company to look for such opportunities is to think in terms of supply chain communities—groups that have a shared interest in collaboration. This can be in business-to-consumer as well as in business-to-business relationships.

Business-to-Consumer Niches

BigWords is an online intermediary for buying and selling college textbooks. Its business model is to "buy books cheap and sell them cheap." Its community is the 76 percent of students who regularly use the Net—and their professors. It rents out books for a course at half the purchase price, sells used books (cheap), and offers a buyback option. Its Tell A Friend program offers 5 percent off your next purchase for steering another student to the BigWords site.

Another program, Tell A Student, turns the site into a value-adding intermediary for professors and students to work together to cut costs of books. The professor lists the books for a course and either 5 percent of the money that students in the course spend is credited toward the teacher's own future purchases or the students get 3 percent off their purchases, even for books that are not on the professor's list.

At first sight, this seems something Amazon or BarnesandNoble.com offer anyway. Certainly, a student can buy the same book directly from either one of them—but only BigWords offers the intermediation value. Together, students and professors get the benefit of price, information, and convenience. Process issues—getting book lists from professors and handling the buyback of books, which is very labor-intensive—keep Amazon and Barnes and Noble out of this innovation.[4] BigWords has created new value via a new style of intermediary in a new niche.

Business-to-Business Hubs

FreeMarkets is a comparable business-to-business example of creation. It offers a hub for large companies to handle contracting for large bids of small items. When United Technologies Corporation (UTC) needed to buy an estimated $24 million of printed circuit boards, it used FreeMarkets, which began by identifying 2,500 qualified contractors. Together, UTC and FreeMarkets winnowed these down; first, to a thousand and then to fifty. These fifty were invited to make bids over the FreeMarkets online site in a highly disciplined bid process that took place over a three-hour period.

The requirements were broken up into twelve lots for a Dutch auction, where the bidding is in reverse, with the lowest bidder winning the auction, in contrast to the more familiar English auction, where the highest bidder wins. The first bid was for $2.25 million. The second bid on this lot was for $2 million; the final one, number forty-two, was for $1.1 million, well under half that of the opening one. By the end of the full auction, UTC got all the boards it needed for a total of $18 million, a 35 percent savings over its estimate, which was based on previous experience.

Since it was set up in 1995, FreeMarkets has handled auctions in over thirty countries and is established in close to sixty industries. United Technologies, one of its part-owners, has carried out more than fifty auctions with FreeMarkets. It reports that it's typically saving 12 percent over its previous contracts. One auction generated 328 bids on ten different lots. FreeMarkets makes its own money from auction fees of around 1 percent of the total value of the auction. This illustrates one of the main principles of the value-adders: leave the customer with most of the value, instead of taking large fees. Even at this low fee, the company's gross profit margins are around 50 percent.

As with Ventro and BigWords, this is far more than just a .com storefront. The added value comes from, first, the clarity of focus on the community to be brought together through the hub and, second, the process innovation that moves the site beyond serving as a simple pass-through hub that just links buyer and seller. If the relationship could be handled by the two parties by direct e-mail, then the hub would provide no added value. And, of course, as we have pointed out many times in *From .com to .profit,* transactions are not in themselves value-adding.

VALUE AND VALUE-ADDING

Value obviously is the issue. In many instances, value comes from information. More and more hubs, both business-to-consumer and business-to-business, have more impact on online transactions than does the transaction owner—the seller of the product or service. Wherever wholesalers, distributors, and dealers play a dominant role in the buyer-manufacturer or buyer–service provider relationship, it's usually because they have superior information and hence can charge higher fees or gain higher margins. A "neutral" intermediary like AutoByTel or AutoWeb takes that advantage away and car dealers can't retain their old information edge. Buyers know the dealers' costs, availability, and prices. The same is the case for airline tickets.

Information isn't in itself value-adding in the sense that customers will pay for it. Very few of the information-based value-adding intermediaries are able to charge a fee. Instead, they make their money through

- Signing up sellers (as with AutoByTel's contracts with dealers)
- Selling information about customer trends and profiles (like Firefly, which gets one-third of its revenues in this way, with another third from licensing its related proprietary databases)
- Online ads that provide links to or referrals for the advertisers (by far the most common source of income)

Obviously, these are only as valuable as their reach and richness of information and their convenience and reliability in providing it. AutoByTel fits these requirements well, as do many of the specialized search tools offered by companies such as MySimon, which locates the best price on the Web for a specified item, or the Real Estate Owners Network, which brings together information on homes for sale by owners but doesn't play any role in the selling process.

Note that a successful value-adding information intermediary is by definition taking away something from someone else who previously had an information edge. This means that companies need to enhance their own information value-adding in their relationships. Otherwise, potential customers will bypass them and rely on an intermediary. That's why, as we mentioned in our discussion of the value imperative of perfecting long-term relationships, providing information on your competitors in order to facilitate comparison shopping is a key step in moving from transaction to relationship. Marshall Industries provides information on manufacturers' prices and inventories that enable buyers to bypass Marshall—but almost all the buyers still stick with Marshall.

Information intermediaries face the challenge of how to charge for their product and services. Few can. Yet when the value comes from relationship, collaboration, and community, companies do find many ways of making money. The most obvious is to bring together trading communities and supply chain partners and handle their interactions in a better way and at a lower cost. Many of the varieties of business-to-business hub provide this advantage: hence their growth in number, market valuation, and transaction volume. At the same time as we are seeing the death of the transaction economy for individual company-to-customer relationships, we are seeing the emergence of a value-adding transaction coordination economy.

Value-Adding Transaction Coordination

The most recent example of the trend toward value-adding transaction co-ordination and one that is beginning to reshape the entire securities trading business is the emergence of electronic communication networks (ECNs). Behind the acronym lies a radical new type of intermediary. His-torically, the intermediary that processes buying and selling of shares has been the NYSE, Amex, and NASDAQ. Their dealers take a "spread" be-tween the price to the buyer and the payment to the seller. ECNs reduce the spread by 30–40 percent. They are specialized services that have been limited by their specialization. A key requirement for trading is "liquidity"— there must be sellers for what buyers are looking for and the reverse.

Island is representative of the new liquid ECNs. Its stated goal is to turn a $3 billion industry into a $1 billion industry by reducing the spreads on stocks quoted on the NASDAQ; those spreads have been a constant concern to government regulators, who see them as far too high and have even suggested that collusion among dealers keeps them high. Island's spread is about 1/15th of a *cent* per share. It has just forty employees, compared to the NYSE's fifteen hundred and NASDAQ's thousand.

Somnet similarly reduces the foreign exchange fees smaller financial institutions must pay. Large banks have the technology and in-house expertise to play in a game where exchange rates can change in seconds, where "spot" and "forward" rates are volatile and complex to evaluate, and where trades are made in multimillion- or even multibillion-dollar blocks, with hedging, derivatives, and other esoterica to compound the complexity. Small banks pay a disproportionately high commission to the large ones. Somnet aggregates their foreign exchange orders and trades in large blocks three times a day.

It's common sense that Island and Somnet represent a major not minor trend across all types of business. They are part of the main drift of business on the Internet: relationship, collaboration, and community. They are growing and will continue to grow, filling in and creating niches and thriving on creativity.

Coordinating Negotiations

Another category of value extends the coordination of relationships and is related to negotiation—getting a better deal. In auctions, for example, hub intermediaries establish new markets. Adauction provides a market space for advertisers to sell spare television commercial time they have booked. Metallink enables producers of, say, steel to advertise and sell excess production instead of having to go through brokers. Priceline is an intermediary for consumers to state a price they are willing to pay for an item and see if it's accepted by an airline, hotel, supermarket, even a car manufacturer.

eCollegebid has created a new vehicle for students to have schools bid to get them, instead of their having to apply for both admission and financial aid. Students enter standard information about grades and test scores—and also state the tuition fees they are willing to pay. Colleges reply within ten days if they accept the "bid." Students then have another thirty days to respond with a yes or no. *Business 2.0* quotes eCollegebid's founder:

"Colleges do a lot of shopping around. They go to college fairs, buy names to send direct mail to, spend tremendous amounts of money on inquiries and prospects, and it's an expensive process. They spend a lot of time working with people who are not going to mature into viable prospects. Through eCollegebid, colleges can look at data, see that the student exceeds the entrance requirements and the amount of money the parents say that they can they can afford to pay is acceptable, so [the colleges] say, yes, we can take that student."[5]

The target is not the Ivy League but the smaller colleges of fewer than a thousand students that attract cash-strapped middle-income families whose children are not eligible for substantial federal aid. The schools that use the service are named only to the students whose bids have been accepted.

Responses from schools have been very varied:

- "Some people are aghast at this. He's been called unethical, but all he's done is leapfrog the marketplace. My first reaction to the site was that I wish I'd thought of it, and my second was that it's a very valuable service." (A dean of admissions at a small college)
- "With all college costs going up, students want the personal attention a private school can offer, at a state-school price." (Another dean)
- "To ask families what they want to pay rather than what they can pay is to open a Pandora's box of financial-aid concerns." (A dean at Caltech, explaining why his university will not be using the service)
- "The College Board, a not-for-profit, membership association that connects students and colleges also shudders at the thought of tuition auctioning. . . . I think this kind of enterprise that focuses on financing is distressing."[6]

The founder counters that college faculty inherently feel that education is a gift and that they have a hard time thinking of education in terms of marketing. "They got it as a gift, and it then becomes their obligation to pass that gift on to the next generation. So the minute you start talking about buying and selling they don't understand, and eCollegebid really heightens that reaction. It takes the position that a student should get into the best college possible, without mortgaging their future to do so."

The service was started in September 1999. It's students and parents—whose responses were not available to be included in the *Business 2.0* article—who will determine if this new form of intermediary succeeds; they are the ones for whom it adds value.

Applications on Tap

One of the most recent forms of new creation of value through hubs is almost sure to transform the entire software industry and the purchasing of software by large, medium, and small companies. This is the explosive growth of "apps-on-tap" through application service providers (ASPs). Here, instead of software packages and related tools being bought, installed, and customized as complete systems, often at a very high price, they are accessed and paid for online as needed. This enables smaller companies to get software they could not otherwise afford, for any company to be accessing the latest version and not have to deal with upgrades and "version control," and then to use only what they want when they want it, instead of having to buy the complete package. Here are a few examples of ASP pricing as of the end of 1999:

- Corio: $25-$295 a month for use of its Web development tools
- Employease: $5–$6 per month per employee for human resources software
- Envoy-I-Con: $29–$59 per user to set up and run online Internet conferences
- Xcollaboration: $100 a year per user for project management software
- Intacct: $67 a month for accounting software. The company estimates that firms with five to five hundred employees spend on average over $2,000 a month for the first year on accounting software and hardware expenses.[7]

A widely reported example of a large-scale ASP hub is the collaboration between Qwest Communications, one of the world's leaders in high-capability Internet telecommunications, SAP, the leader in enterprise resource planning (ERP) software, and Hewlett-Packard. SAP is notoriously expensive to purchase and complex to implement. Accordingly, it's been the preserve of large firms. Qwest provides the network, SAP the software, and HP the hardware for a new pay-as-you-use service. SAP-on-Tap saves users hundreds of dollars. This is not the only benefit. Others include speed of response to the need for new applications, better management and forecasting of technology costs, reductions in in-house storage, and fewer hardware components, plus access to the scale, service, and support advantages that this giant "hosting" CyberCenter service provides.

ASPs are the future of the software industry and of the next generation of Internet uses. They are popping up everywhere. It may take time for CIOs in Fortune 1000 companies to adopt them; several reports in late 1999 showed that many CIOs are wary of switching from their established, reliable, and well-understood purchase, development, and operational practices. But ASPs and their near relations—Business SPs, Wholesale SPs, and Functional SPs—will inevitably take over from the license-and-install tradition.

THE MANAGEMENT AGENDA: INTERMEDIARIES AND VALUE

Value-adding hubs and intermediaries are the very core of the future in more and more areas of Internet business. It's that simple. Firms have three options:

1. *Create a position as a value-adding intermediary.* Doing so, as Ariba, Ventro, AutoByTel, and many others have, demands real evidence in the business model of value-adding, plenty of capital, marketing, and speed. It's where much of .profit entrepreneurship and innovation is focused. It requires, at minimum, that the company:

- Be clear about the community to be brought together through the hub.
- Set up a win-win via special-purpose portals.
- Use innovation to move the site beyond being simply a pass-through hub that links buyer and seller.
- Add value through information, coordination, collaboration, and community.

2. *Use value-adding intermediaries.* It's simply foolish for any company to forgo value by ignoring the new intermediaries, especially in their own logistics and supply chain coordination. The payoffs are proven and large. Direct price savings in procurement of goods and services are 10–30 percent, with reach to a larger range of customers and suppliers. Reduction of capital investment and overhead, support, and administrative expenses extend the savings as well as streamlining and speeding up operations.

3. *Respond to value-adding intermediaries by adding value in your own services.* Car dealers and car manufacturers are having to respond to online intermediaries like AutoByTel and AutoWeb. The more they offer the same range of information, choices of supply and suppliers, and good prices, the better their chance of building and sustaining relationships. The less they do so, of course, the more likely it is that they will be victims of those intermediaries.

Create, use, respond—they all work. What is not an option is to ignore the value-adding intermediaries. That is, not if you want your company to thrive in the future.

11

IMAGINE ... WHAT'S NEXT?

Prepare for the future: Engineer and imagineer—or disappear.

The final chapter of any good book, especially one extolling a vision of the future, always looks forward, extends that vision a bit, and makes a few provocative predictions. Since this is a book about a vision of the Internet economy and where it is going, here's a bold prediction in the form of a final imperative:

The .com phase of the Net is over; to win in .profit, companies will have to make a basic strategic decision to either dominate their own ecosystem or be brokered out as the dominant plug-in to other ecosystems.

To succeed in either event, companies will have to leverage e-services to create a total customer experience, making it impossible for their customers to defect to competitors one click away. They will need to take full advantage of new efficiencies on the Internet to create virtual communities of common interest that unshackle their members from the PC and interconnect anywhere, anytime by the Web-enabled mobile device of choice. The next Internet revolution will not just be about disruptive technologies but also about disruptive business models.

This raises a fundamental question: Can a company with a past reinvent its future? This is a question more relevant to the Fortune 2000 than to the .com start-up that begins from nothing. For blue chip enterprises, midsize companies, and small business entrepreneurs alike—the old rules don't apply. If 1 percent of the overall economy moving to the Internet can cause the kind of disruption we saw to an established company like Procter & Gamble (which saw its market cap drop 30 percent one day in March 2000), imagine the kind of disruption these companies will have to confront when the Internet economy reaches just 3 percent of overall business.

REINVENTING FOR THE FUTURE WAVE

Established bricks-and-mortar companies like P&G, and even more so high-tech companies like HP, have to practice change management at every corner; they have to reinvent themselves over and over to prepare for the next "new new thing." These stalwart companies have to realize that the .com era is over. As Morgan Stanley's Mary Meeker sees it:

"Up until now, we've had waves, about one a year, and each with its own poster child: UUnet was infrastructure; Netscape was net software; Yahoo! was portals; Amazon was e-commerce; eBay was C-to-C; Healtheon was B-to-B. People focused on one thing. But now there are lots of new things simultaneously: wireless, ASPs, Europe, Asia, logistics. . . . Last year's theme goes by the wayside, but there's always a new story. So you have to assume that capital flows into the sector that remains robust."[1]

And so, our prediction: the next big wave will have very little to do with companies selling their products on the Internet. Amazon.com has won C-to-B e-commerce and eBay has won C-to-C e-commerce. And even though Healtheon and other supply chain automators deserve credit for helping create the B-to-B wave, the next big wave will go beyond optimizing the supply chain. That's important but not enough to sustain the inevitable shift to .profit. The next big wave on the Internet will be about econets and how—paralleling ecosystems in nature—companies that make one slight change will affect the entire business ecosystem.

What are econets? They are what *Red Herring* calls "the economic networks of the future" that will influence how businesses will be "organized, structured and operated" for decades to come. According to Andrew

"Flip" Filipowski, founder of Divine Interventures, econets will become the conglomerates of the next century. They are "the quickest means of spinning out and building up Internet businesses" for bricks-and-mortar companies. And it won't be just Internet companies. Filipowski believes the econet model will allow companies to lock up intellectual capital, institutional relationships, and deal flow, creating mini economies within new corporate structures.[2]

The leading companies of tomorrow, whether they are the Global 2000 or the Silicon Valley start-up, will be confronted with two fundamental choices:

- Make a play to capture the entire ecosystem in which your company subsists.
- Create significant enough value that can brokered out to other ecosystems on the Net, making it impossible for a relevant econet to succeed without plugging your company into its value chain.

To simplify the choice companies have to make down to a brief analogy: do you want to be a Yahoo or a Mapquest? Yahoo has created a tremendous amount of gravity, a giant attractor, into which plug-in features get pulled. Mapquest, on the other hand—equally successful but in a very different business model—is a valuable component that has become ubiquitous for a generic portal or even most Web sites that want users to be able to do geographic mapping. In this sense, Mapquest wants to be brokered out to as many Web sites as possible to sustain its business model. On the other hand, Yahoo wants the reverse—sticky eyeballs to create enough critical mass in one place to charge premiums for its real estate.

Another equally bold prediction: companies that get it right will make more money from the .profit econet business model than they ever will from .com e-commerce. The main reason? Econets will make it possible to extract at least 35 percent greater efficiencies than any business model previously on the Internet.

How will these econets manifest themselves? They will flourish in three fundamental areas:

1. Econets around consumers (memo to Yahoo—huge opportunity!)
2. Econets around the enterprise (ditto to SAP!)
3. Econets around your competitors (memo to self!)

That last one is perhaps the most interesting and significant. But back to our central question: can a company with a past reinvent its future? It can. The following pages focus on several success stories happening today among traditional blue chip companies who are leading the way to the .profit econet era. We'll look at some examples of econets in each of the three key market segments: consumers, enterprises, and competitors.

Econets for Consumers

The first phase of the Internet, in which companies sought to .com themselves, a sort of *Field of Dreams* strategy ("If you build it, they will come.") has reached its apex. Now your e-commerce Web site is six, seven, eight clicks down on a generic portal like AOL. If your product has strong brand equity in the physical world, what are you going to do? That's serious brand erosion. As of April 2000, there were a billion unique documents on 5 million unique sites on the World Wide Web: how can consumers find you? The answer is not to .com yourself but rather to wrap your product with services and create an econet around the community of common interests.

Our first example of a customer econet is an exciting one: Swatch. With 500 million watches on wrists around the world, you would think Swatch is in the watch business. Think again. Swatch is in the brand fashion business and owns the metaphor for time. If you go to the Swatch Web site, you may see the obligatory photo gallery of the latest, greatest watch designs, but what Swatch is really doing on the Web is building value around its products by creating a borderless time zone, BMT or Biel Mean Time, that observes its own orthodoxy of time at any point on the globe. The World Wide Web knows no artificial geopolitical boundaries. The next generation of ecosystem players, the generation-i, want to wear their access device as "skin." Swatch wants them to make an emotional connection to the brand. It is doing that in part by building an online experience around the value proposition of their products. Soon, Swatch will go even further to create the wrist power zone—a Web-enabled watch that can be brokered to by HP's e-speak software, its platform for simplifying business on the Internet. It can create a virtual on-the-go bazaar for transactional services. The latest music video clip, video archives of the Olympics, transportation services—whatever they can squeeze onto the wristtop.

HP and the Swatch Group recently forged a partnership to build the world's first wristwatch that delivers on the promise of the wireless Internet. As HP CEO Carly Fiorina said when she announced the partnership during her speech at COMDEX '99: "Swatch will now be more than just a fashion statement, more than just a reliable timepiece. You'll be able to access e-services through it."

Now, imagine this vision, in which Swatch is creating an ecosystem around its core competency (brand management of uniquely designed watches) and brokering it to talk to something like myalert.com. That's a recipe for instant gratification—a marketer's dream. According to CEO and founder Jorge Mata, myalert.com can create the following scenario over a mobile device: "You want to know who's winning the Grand Prix? Myalert.com finds you the answer. Now, do you want to buy a T-shirt with the driver's name on it? No problem. Want to buy stock in the driver's racing company? Easy. Want to be alerted to tickets for the next race? A snap."[3]

When Swatch captures transaction revenues in this way will it (a) sell the watches? (b) give them away? or (c) pay you to wear one? What would you do?

This of course signals one of the big trends that econets will enable: wireless services, a topic that we will get back to later. But even now it's clear that the power of the Web coming to you on your wristwatch makes it pretty tough for the consumer to defect to some other econet. As the Realtors say, it's all down to location, location, location—or maybe it should be Wrist, Pocket, Eyeglasses.

Another example of an econet for consumers is FedEx—synonymous for reliable delivery. You would expect fedex.com to have lots of information about shipping prices and of course how to track and trace your shipment. Rob Carter, CIO of FedEx, has another vision—he wants to be the ubiquitous plug-in so that anytime, anywhere, on the PC-accessed Web or from a mobile device, a consumer clicks on "ship it," FedEx can broker its services for that transaction. On the fly, in any given econet, leveraging e-speak's dynamic brokering language. Of course FedEx builds greater brand equity than just simply .comming itself, because the e-commerce consumer is touched by the brand when the package arrives at the door—on time, of course.

One more consumer econet example that emphasizes the power of dynamically brokered e-services, this time for digital media content. Helsinki Telephone, the main telecommunications service provider in mobile-phone-crazy Finland, decided to e-speak–enable its wireless phone service to discover and deliver digital media content directly to the handset. One application involves students of Helsinki University who are able to broker through SMS (short messaging services that allows users to send text to each other instantly) and share with each other the latest music clips. What music marketer would not kill to own the ecosystem of hit-crazy teens? Take it one step further and make the device compatible with MP3 (a compression format that allows bulky music files to be stored and swapped over the Internet) and pretty soon, it's "game over." Helsinki is reinventing itself to be a digital media content broker, not a telephone company, and this has little to do with a PC-based, Web site–based e-commerce business model.

Econets for Enterprises

Let's turn to the second major econet category we've identified: econets for the enterprise. Logistics, relationships, channels, cost structures, branding, value-adding intermediary—those are the last things you might associate with a building supply company. But that doesn't mean that "old" companies can't and aren't coming up with new business models. One of the top five home improvement chains is planning to build the ultimate business econet around the ultimate commodity products. In the .com world, your local hardware store Web site would be an online shopping mall for wood, paint, and nails. A recipe for snoozeville in anyone's book . . . can you imagine how boring browsing different sizes of nails would be? Instead, this chain is determined to be an e-services player by creating an ecosystem around the people—carpenters, contractors, carpet layers, and others—who buy its products.

The point is that their most valuable customer—the customer that brings in the most profit—is not the guy in the store on Sunday but the small contractor buying in bulk to prepare for a job at your house. In the store, the contractor is a customer like anybody else; on the Web site, the contractor is both part of a wider community and part of a dynamic relationship with the company. A contractor comes to your house with a laptop and sizes out the deck for new planking. The site provides automatic sizing, online help, cost estimates, what materials will be needed, what the schedule should be, and any likely snags to look out for. There's an instant confirmation of availability of items from the suppliers. The site asks where, when, and how the items should be delivered, with the option to receive them all at the same time or on a just-in-time basis. After all, who really likes queuing up in a line of trucks to pick up materials? Why not save forty-five minutes by having them delivered to the job? If the contractor needs a plumber or an electrician—someone from the wider community—the site posts the job and in effect acts as a labor exchange service. Finally why should the guy in the store on Sunday fill out that little card saying "Plumber needed" and stick it on to the felt board at the back of the store when an agent will post it on the site and contractors will bid for his business? When this goes live, is the company still a shop selling things—or is it a very profitable Application Services Provider with a lot of wood, paint, and nails on hand?

And now, for another household name—Ford Motor Company. Its enterprise ecosystem also included employees. In this age of scarce skilled human resources, how do you win the talent wars? As we mentioned back in Chapter Two, Ford has taken dramatic steps and made alliances to this end. Every employee, all 350,000, many members of the United Auto Workers—very much an offline, old world union representing an extremely fragmented industry (and there isn't too much Net access on the assembly line)—will now, thanks to an innovative business model from HP and PeoplePC, receive a PC, printer, and Internet access at home all for $5 per month. Think about it. . . . That's about a fifth of the monthly cost of AOL access—and it includes all the equipment!

In addition to all the critical information Ford needs to get to its employees, information that before cost a lot of money and time to deliver in physical formats, Ford can facilitate communications and collaboration among employees, from employees to management, from employees to suppliers. Additionally, what better way to build employee loyalty than by clearing out an entire section of the home PC desktop to consolidate icons of service providers who, through the power of leverage and critical mass, are able to offer Ford employees attractive discounts and loyalty programs.

This also proves that just because you're an Old World company with large numbers of employees doesn't mean you can't reinvent yourself with new business models for the Internet economy. This will increasingly become the model for large companies of all industries, not just with employees, but also with customers and partners. Why stop at every employee of every company, why not give a free PC, printer, and Internet access with every car or even every gold credit card? After all it's not the PC you're giving them—it's the unique bundle of your services on that PC, or appliance, or webphone, or watch that you are really handing out. You thought the Sabre business model was clever? You ain't seen nothin' yet.

Econets for Competitors

Finally, we get to the third big indicator of econets, and those are econets for competitors. Again, let's turn our eyes to Detroit and Ford. In the last big wave in the B-to-B space, the generic, horizontal e-commerce portals successfully automated and Web-enabled basic supply chain functions such as order entry and procurement. But that was then. The econet of the future will be a virtual community around a common vertical market, trading hubs built around meaningful content, even microhubs for niche markets, for example, steel tube market players and not just steel in general. In this case, Ford made a game-over play for its own vertical trading community when it invited and secured the three largest players in its ecosystem, representing 50 percent of all procurement in the auto industry.

Imagine if in the mid-1990s, someone said that the world largest automotive companies, long-standing rivals, would sit down and build a Web business together—and that they would share resources. That would have been unthinkable. Now, because of the Internet's power to remove barriers, it is happening. This is probably the most dramatic story that is imaginable in supply chain econets today and into the future.

The impetus for this project was the realization, by Ford's top management, that the Internet was going to change the car business. Where consumers traditionally had preconfigured cars available to them that had been placed into dealerships by the company, which spent massive marketing dollars to stand out, the Internet has now given the consumers the power to choose the products they want from a Web site . . . including automobiles. Consumers are demanding more choice and even more customization.

For Ford that meant shifting from the mind-set of being an Old World industrial company to being a New World consumer products company—meaning more customization and consumer-driven options and therefore fewer unsold preconfigured cars sitting on a dealer's lot. The problem was how to support production that was going to be subjected to more and more rapid change. At the same time, there were inefficiencies in the century-old automotive supply chain that needed to be squeezed out in order to maintain an attractive price for consumers. Ford recognized that the squeeze was going to happen; the choice was to be part of it or to be left behind. That's a pretty heavy conclusion for the company that typified the industrial age better than any other manufacturer in the world. The significance here is that Ford is spinning this out as an independent entity, and it is partnering in the exchange with arch rivals GM and DaimlerChrysler to extend the model for the entire auto sector. Why? Because it makes sense for the entire industry. If you are a supplier forced to use three different systems, one for each company, that would be ridiculous. Maintaining three systems would be expensive and drive up the price of doing business. In the Internet age we run on common standards because it benefits the entire industry tremendously.

In terms of results it is still too early for exact figures on what this means. As a start, the carmakers seem to agree that squeezing out inefficiencies could reduce the cost of producing a vehicle by up to a thousand dollars. Some benefits are already apparent from the supply chain at Ford. They have already moved $16 billion in purchasing onto the Web. They have also integrated the supply chain with their design and engineering units. The ability to share information about component needs in real time across the Internet has already shaved time off the process of designing and producing a new model. Where once it took at least three years to roll out a new model, that process has now been shortened to less than two. That means lower costs and faster time to market with the vehicles that consumers want. That's how you become a customer-driven company. And Ford is looking to build the relationship beyond selling a car, such as more after-sale service. The gravity Ford is creating will set the stage for the company to make more money and drive stronger loyalty by wrapping their products with e-services available through their own econet.

But perhaps the most important results are the changes that are taking place in the culture of Ford. Could you imagine a decade ago that Ford would embark on anything this ambitious without having a complete, locked-down plan? What it takes to move forward in the New World is leadership and the understanding that the technology is extremely flexible. If you try something new and it doesn't work, it's easier to change and implement a new plan than to do nothing at all.

Forming one of these new competitor-to-competitor econets is not so easy. For a start you have to form a new company with your competitors. Bitter rivals in the morning have to sit down, partner, and strategize in the afternoon. Employees with an appetite for risk and a healthy frustration with the way your company traditionally works have to be selected to leave the mother ship and join the new economy company. HR policies have to be ripped up and an aggressive stock equity program introduced in record time to attract and retain these employees. (After all, once you've had a taste of a .com in disguise, why not leave and join the real thing? You've always wanted that Ferrari. . . .) If you think for one moment that it's "not right" that twenty-six-year-olds can rake in millions in these entities, then you've lost before you've started.

And who will own the company? An Internet incubator? Maybe, but what have they really got other than money, buildings, and a PE ratio of 700-plus? An Internet-savvy VC? That's probably not the type of board meeting you're used to. How about a procurement software company? After all, they seem to know how to do these things. So far in the early days of vertical econets the software companies have indeed owned the majority stakes with the same VCs who invested in them also sitting at the table. Our prediction is that this will change and change fast. The big C-to-C econets will be owned by the companies who put their transactions through the econet for the simple reason that these new companies will be worth more than the sum of the members. The winners will be those who can move quickly and who can partner. Are these your company's core competencies?

PROFITING FROM THE
TOTAL CUSTOMER EXPERIENCE

In the next phase of the Internet, in which an econet-driven transactional services economy places even greater demands on the corporate network, a customer's online experience will define the company's brand. In a sense, the company's technology becomes its business proposition. Successful companies on the Web today are emulating many of the big players in the offline world by building e-services around products. In the next couple of years, even those e-services will become commoditized and customers will expect the ultimate experience to earn their loyalty.

The .profit era will signal the revenge of the big players on the Internet, the Nordstroms and the Wal-Marts, because they understand how to stage a rich, compelling experience and apply it to a technology environment that can create or extinguish a brand in the blink of an eye. Even the poster children of the .com phase of the Internet will have to compete on this field. The speed with which decisions are made online requires companies to adjust their own behavior accordingly and deliver traditional and online service to a "cash-rich, time poor" customer with greater flexibility and innovation. This "experience" economy will require new econets encompassing ultimate experiences for customers and employees, individual shareholders and institutional investors, trading partners and suppliers. It will require companies to build loyalty six times faster on the Internet, making it impossible for a customer to defect. And it will force companies to view downtime as brand erosion and place a greater premium on building an IT infrastructure that is up and running all the time.

To win in the .profit game, companies will have to address the following questions themselves or with partners or through an econet relationship in order to deliver a total customer experience:

- Do our customers always get first-class treatment?
- Can we ensure that the moment a visitor to our site switches from browsing to buying, systems will perform flawlessly?
- In a bandwidth-restricted world, do we have a strategy for allocating that bandwidth to those customers with the most benefit?
- How do we ensure that each customer gets the right level of service?
- Do we know how to manage all the components, from end to end, that make up that experience, even if we don't control either end?
- Who will be ultimately responsible for ensuring the performance of the Web?

Keep these questions in mind as we take a look at how one well-known retailer added a personal touch to its customers' total e-tailing experience.

The Lands' End catalog company takes pride in being completely focused on taking care of the customer. Talk to anyone at Lands' End and they'll quote their leader, who says, "First take care of the customer, and everything else will take care of itself." Yet when Lands' End added the Web to its sales channel, its management soon realized there was a problem. Although the Web was a great self-service model and had great graphic capabilities, it was doing a poor job with human relations. This is a business issue. How can a company that prides itself on personal interaction bring that interaction to the Web?

Imagine this. A potential customer is shopping on the Web and has a question about a style, a color . . . whatever. There was no way to ask a question. Sure, customers could call an 800 number and explain what they were looking at. But most customers still have a single phone line and dial up to get on the Web—so they can't ask questions and Web shop at the same time. A shopper who became frustrated might not complete a transaction. To Lands' End the problem was evident—60 percent of all the online "shopping carts" left without purchases. The people at Lands' End needed to understand what customers were thinking and be able to communicate with them. What was needed was a direct channel for help that was as personal as a phone call. In addition, Lands' End was somewhat blind about where questions were arising on the Web site. So it decided that it was time to use another aspect of the Web to close the loop.

The solution Lands' End is using is relatively simple. Leverage the existing investment in Web applications and augment and reinforce human expertise with a closed-loop integration to make sure that Web customer is never dropped. It took adding software that could immediately let a dedicated team of agents know that a customer had a question and respond in real time.

The application also provided the ability to "push" pages out to customers much as a sales assistant would show merchandise in a main street storefront environment. We call this class of applications customer relationship management or CRM software—a category that is growing exponentially and absolutely key to succeeding in the .profit e-services era. As we see the Internet and the voice telephone begin to merge, customer service will improve and costs of operating call centers will decrease.

The results for Lands' End are a continuation of its heritage of extremely personalized service. The brand promise is extended to the Web, maintaining customer loyalty. This loyalty is important because the cost of acquiring new customers is five to ten times that of retaining a current customer.

Lands' End's shift from .com to .experience made an enormous difference: Web commerce went from $61 million to $120 million in fiscal 2000. More important, Lands' End has ensured its place in the New World economy.

Another illustration of how to make serving customers a total experience comes from another non-techie. Stelios Haji-Ioannou founded EasyJet, a British equivalent of Southwest Airlines. It combines low-cost airfares with quality customer service. He quickly saw the value of the Internet as a low-cost and convenient booking service substitute for call centers, as an alternative to reliance on travel agents (and their commissions) and for using the major airlines' reservation systems (and paying their fees). Thirty-five percent of EasyJet's tickets are booked over the Net at a cost of pennies versus around $20 through phone service. EasyJet now commands 55 percent of Internet airline reservation bookings, the highest of any airline in the world.

Stelios is using the Internet as a vehicle for combining customer convenience through self-service with EasyJet's own cost reduction through self-service—the fundamental win-win combination that the Net enables. In addition, he is using the Net to create a new community-centered business: the Easy Everything Internet Café, a bravura initiative that makes his company look like a baby gorilla stretching its muscles. He spotted what may not be obvious to Internet players whose managers all have personal computers, live by e-mail, and are comfortable with technology. This comfort—and access to computers—is not widespread; it is enjoyed by only a tiny minority in the UK. Stelios cites the fact that, in his view, a majority of people will never be able to afford a PC, printer, and Internet access—but all of them would love to use the Internet.

Hence the Café. Each Café accommodates around four hundred people. There are currently four located in the center of London with an additional seventy-five locations planned throughout Europe. The Café operates 24 × 7—all day, every day. Outside each Café, there is typically a line of up to eighty people waiting to get in. Once inside, each customer pays a fixed price of £1 an hour—about $1.60—for simple access to the Internet. In May 2000, Stelios implemented a new pricing policy for non–prime time hours: £1 for four hours of Internet access. Amazingly, Stelios' Cafés are already profitable. This is Easy Everything: customers don't need to know about browsers, Windows, operating systems, modems, or even computers. They just sit down, log on, and enjoy.

But what Stelios is really doing is preparing his attack on the High Street. His vision is a physical venue for shoppers to access their own personal portal. In other words, he's enabling consumers to build their own shopping experience in the real world while leveraging the e-services benefits of the virtual world. Why not visit the stores in London's central shopping area and check out records you'd like to buy, or look at books, VCRs, or whatever. Then come back to the Café and sit down and see the deal Easy Everything can get for you. Through the wonders of the Internet and the obsession for every company to sell online, you too will get that book, sweater, or washing machine for a lower price than in the store! And you don't have to lug the goods home with you; they'll be delivered. Making money doesn't have to be based on complicated business models, it can be based on $1.60 for four hours' access to the greatest wonder of the world.

Will the Easy Everything Internet Café turn out to be a big winner? We think it will, but that's not really the issue. The Café is a powerful new business model that can't be dismissed. It's also not "technology"—though it relies on technology as its identity and service base. And if it is successful, it will fracture the business models of London retailers—not because Easy Everything will take huge amounts of business away from them but because the business model will.

Music is a good example. In fact it's a great example because here is one airline executive likely to compete with another (Richard Branson) using the business models of the Internet. Box 11.1 illustrates what is, for now, a fictional example of a scenario that might, just might, play out. It's a scenario based on a trend written up by *Fortune* columnist and venture capitalist Stewart Alsop in "Bye Bye Music Business," an article based on the archaic and rapidly changing world of music copyright law.[4]

Box 11.1. Easy Raider

What if Stelios were to open up an Easy Everything Internet Café right next to a Virgin Megastore? (Which, by the way, he is doing.) What if he were to install compressor personal jukeboxes—a 4.6-gigabyte hard disk in a small portable box capable of downloading and storing about eighty hours of music, or about a hundred CDs, free over the Internet—as a high-bandwidth network device in every store, charging only for the usage or renting out the drive? These devices are becoming widespread now. You can buy them for about $500 each and load your entire stack of CDs onto a solid-state device that fits into your pocket. Students are using them in the tens of thousands to listen to their music while they skate, shop, run, ski, whatever.

And, while you're in the store downloading your CDs, what if you could access a Web page powered by napster.com—an Internet service that finds music for you on other people's compressor personal jukeboxes that are connected to PCs anywhere on the Net? What this means is that you can search and find any track or combination of tracks providing just one person to whom you are connected had stored it to one of these devices.

What if people then started going into cities like London and spending two hours in extremely high cost-per-square-foot retail outlets, the aforementioned Megastores, browsing CDs, sampling music, and then walking straight past the till and to the store next door (Easy Everything Internet Café) to search for the music and download it to their personal jukebox? All for $1.60 for four hours.

All of sudden, Stelios has a disruptive business model that gives him a competitive advantage. Who's breaking the law in this scenario? Not Stelios—compressor personal jukeboxes are readily available. Not Napster—it's just pointing people to where the music is. How about the individuals? That is not clear—some people say they are, some not. But even if they are, how is the law going to be enforced? You can't very well go after every individual musicjacker and make millions of house arrests. That's like sending out the police to arrest people who tear the tags off their mattresses and pillows.

The point is, as a decrepit Old World wall starts to crumble, millions of people start doing things the new way, en masse, and you're faced with an unstoppable market. Those will be the rules of the New World. The smart companies will either start a stampede or get trampled. And indeed it has started: In April 2000, BMG Entertainment (the parent company of Arista, RCA, and other labels) announced that it will begin selling music digitally over the Internet, using copyright-protection technologies from three different companies. In making this announcement, BMG acknowledged that it can't wait for the perfect copyright-protection system: it has to make it work *now*.[5]

WHAT LIES AHEAD?
MAJOR IMPACTS, MAJOR OPPORTUNITIES

Here is an easy prediction: customers will access e-services through their cell phones as much as through their personal computers. Wireless IP (Internet Protocol—the shared communication language for Internet hardware and software to link to each other) and mobile tools will mark the next major set of developments in electronic commerce. Companies who understand this basic tenet—that the future ultimate experience in the .profit econet will require mobility—will win, period.

To understand the magnitude of this shift, consider that according to International Data Corporation, worldwide mobile devices will lead Net-appliance shipments by 2004, when they're forecast to grab 37 percent of the market; further, IDC adds that the worldwide value of these Net-enabled appliances will reach almost $18 billion by 2004.[6]

Mobile e-services will transform many areas of business-to-consumer commerce for some very simple reasons: People prefer to use the phone, all other things being equal. When the phone becomes a device with high bandwidth, high-resolution display, and a full browser, it will be a preferred customer tool. Today, the PC is, in effect, the company-mandated tool. To access Internet services customers now have two basically different choices: telephone call center and PC. Soon, they will have the benefits of both. The Nokia Communicator is the leader here—and in a sense already obsolete. Motorola, Sprint, Ericcson, Qualcomm, and others are marketing Internet phones. At press time, they remain limited in their features and speed, but that will change very soon. Amazon and AOL have already implemented alliances with wireless service providers, and E*Trade sees the mobile phone as your broker.

Wireless opens up many opportunities for service at the customer moment of value. It takes the technology where the customer is, at the very time that customer is interested in a service. It extends $24 \times 7 \times 365$ to $24 \times 7 \times 365 \times$ anywhere.

Mobility always has advantages over fixed location, but the fixed-location computer has had advantages of functions and bandwidth. That is guaranteed to change now that fully modern digital wireless networks are replacing the muddle of fragmented analog and limited local digital services. Europe is already at that point, through GSM. The United States will surely catch up before long. Already a wireless "protocol" is being widely applied in Europe that transmits full Web pages (wireless application protocol or WAP standard). It's showing up in the United States, too, with limited availability.

Wireless technology places the system complexity in the provider network, not at the user end. The most difficult step in configuring a mobile phone is waiting for the battery to charge; obviously there is no need for toll-free cell phone help desks.

Internet telephony—"Voice over IP"—is well beyond the demonstration stage. Quality of service is getting closer and closer to the level that the public phone service providers aim for before they move to full-scale deployment; already it's superior to analog cell phone service. Voice over IP changes everything for telecommunications. For electronic commerce, it makes call centers and Internet the same customer interaction channel.

Wireless IP appliances turn your PDA and cell phone into your personal relationship contact point. And, of course, they transform your personal logistics and channel management. Think you've got scaling problems in the PC-dominated .com world? Imagine the tsunami that will hit your IT shop when twenty-five times as many devices as PCs start hitting your site.

The combination of devices and brokered services will in effect remove the @ sign, the implication of a fixed address, in Web addresses. This New World is site independent and location independent: it's the

World Wide Everywhere. As we move from .com to .profit, what areas will have major impacts resulting from all these trends?

- *Product brand equity.* The world of dynamic e-service brokers and agents communicating across the Web to any and every type of access appliance means the shattering of product brand equity. How do we know? Ask a group of people if any of them have bought a book via Amazon recently. Hands go up. Then ask if they can remember the publisher's name. Most hands go down. Take a look at Priceline's success with airline tickets. Priceline is the brand—not the airline, which the buyer doesn't specify. Then look at the B-to-B hubs that streamline procurement and find a way to differentiate office supply products versus the hub that provides the coordination of buying and selling.

- *Advertising and sales force.* Traditional advertising and sales forces will be disintermediated as much as travel agents and car dealers are experiencing already. In the world of dynamic brokers, personalization, and customization, what will advertising and selling mean? We'll have to see. As just one example, shopping bots are already increasing the percentage of customer inquiries that turn into sales from 1 percent to 10 percent.

- *Fixed pricing.* Fixed pricing will be a quaint artifact of the past. Give it away, e-services, auctions, reverse auctions, bartering, and group purchase power will dominate. The purchaser is in control and will here on out dictate the price threshold.

- *The leader-laggard gap.* The gap between the value imperative leaders and followers will widen to the degree that we will witness the auctioning off of many Fortune 1000 and midsized players who've missed out on the .profit game. At present, the heavy investment costs for funding this value imperative so drown out profits that traditional companies with their average 5–6 percent margin look healthy. With today's economy, many of the new competitors won't make it to .profit, but those that do— as AOL, Yahoo, and Cisco show already—are literally entrenched in a different economic landscape.

Beyond these, the real impact hasn't even begun. The major political, social, economic, and global impacts of the Internet are yet unforeseen, but indubitably will be quite significant. Europe, Asia, and Latin America didn't play much in the early .com game. They're moving at Internet speed now (as is the small fraction of Africa that is not being devastated by wars, famine, and disaster). The online 1 percent of the economy was built on slow telecommunications and expensive personal computers. The next surge will rely on broadband and appliances many times faster and many times cheaper and of course vastly more mobile—wires will become superfluous. The "World Wide" Web has been a misnomer; it's largely been the worldwide Web—call it W3—with as much real, world-spanning scope as the baseball World Series. It's now moving to W5—a *worldwide*-worldwide Web covering all geographies.

The level of technology innovation occurring to bring about these impacts clearly opens up many new opportunities in every single one of the six business imperatives that we have presented as the templates for a successful .profit business model design:

1. *Perfect Your Logistics.* E-services extends logistics capabilities enormously: it's like adding a massive set of agents roaming the Net, negotiating, looking for deals, checking changes in price and availability, and putting together proposals. This is as big a leap ahead from today's business-to-business online hubs as those hubs are from traditional paper and phone transactions.
2. *Cultivate Your Long-Term Customer Relationships.* Similarly, e-services add even more customization and personalization to relationships.
3. *Harmonize Your Channels on the Customer's Behalf.* As for the imperative of channel harmony, all this looks like a very new channel in itself—perhaps we could call it the "dynamic broker network."
4. *Build a Power Brand for Your Business.* E-services also opens up branding opportunities, especially in financial services, which rely on agents acting on your behalf—insurance agents, mortgage brokers, bank account relationship managers, and others. The transaction-centered bank Web sites and call centers of today are among the weakest elements of online business. There is as yet no equivalent of Amazon, eBay, or Yahoo in the consumer banking sector nor an Ariba, CommerceNet, or GE TPN in the business sector. There will be a financial e-services power brand within a year of this book's publication date to fulfill natural demand—and it won't necessarily be a bank.
5. *Transform Your Capital and Cost Structures.* E-services is part of a complete redefinition of the economics of business—.profit squared. We've

seen how companies like Cisco and AOL are cash flow machines, how a Dell generates massive profits on minimal invested balance sheet capital, and how eBay and Yahoo have operating margins of 70 percent or more. That's the advantage of a revenue stream based on digital transactions and a cost structure based on software and telecommunications. And that's all done today with .com era technology. E-services is a step shift up the economics curve. The cost of providing all this is pennies per customer interaction. AOL showed that a $5 billion online firm can be built that generates over a billion dollars of cash flow. Somewhere out there in the near future a business model will be created based on a $5 billion company with $4 billion of cash flow.

6. *Become a Value-Adding Intermediary—or Use One.* This imperative is an obvious e-services target. Indeed, many of today's innovations reflect this concept's dynamic foundations: the business-to-business auctions, trading hubs, and new supply chain value networks. All of these are enhanced and extended by the ability to create a software-to-software and data-to-data set of conversations that work nonstop across the Web. This trend will facilitate very rapid development of agents, bots, objects, applets—all the self-contained, flexible, and small units of software that make it easy to customize sites in the way that, say, Schwab does with its MySchwab and others do to develop and maintain dynamic product catalogs (Broadvision), build supply chain hubs (Ariba), and to manage dynamic pricing (Priceline).

Innovations are clearly speeding up. Consider, for instance, that it took radio thirty-eight years to reach 50 million users; television, thirteen years; and the Internet, a mere four years! And we all know that the speed will increase and the growth will continue. The U.S. Commerce Department sees consumer traffic on the Internet doubling every hundred days and estimates that a billion people will be on the Internet by 2002.

While Old World businesses are driven by process, New World businesses are driven by the need to improve relationships with customers, whether those customers are partners, employees, or consumers. The Internet is the great enabler for bringing people together. The challenge for all of us is this: How to harness the inherent ability of the Internet to affect positive change for the betterment of society?

BEYOND ENGINEERING:
IMAGINEERING FOR THE NEXT GENERATION

Reaching back to HP's inventive heritage, we have begun to take a page out of the book of our first customer, the Walt Disney Co., and hold "imagineering" sessions with our field and consultants, to look way out into the future and imagine what's truly possible to make the Web work for people, to make it warmer, friendlier, easier to use, accessible to all. To make the Web the digital uniter, not the digital divider. These HP "imagineers" will be the catalysts for change in the e-services market of the future and for HP's culture. Can a company with a past reinvent its future? HP imagineers, in the research lab and out, are helping answer that question with a resounding yes!

For every business, the job is to bring all this mobile appliance, Web-centric vision together into real world-scenarios that we'll all see within two years.

The Swatch Internet watch we mentioned earlier is the first of the next-generation "context-aware" Web devices being developed at HP Labs. Although initially the appliances will require a password or PIN, eventually they will use biometrics—fingerprint, iris, face, or voice recognition—to identify the user. They'll use GPS or other positioning technology to determine location. And they'll contain sensors that will provide information—temperature, light, sound, motion—about the environment.

Users control how much information they share about themselves. One context-aware device in the works at HP Labs is BadgePAD, a smart badge that might be used in a work setting. In a hospital, for instance, doctors could pick up a BadgePAD when they arrive at work. The badge would know what's going on around the physician because Web servers would be embedded throughout the facility. Everyone else—nurses, orderlies, technicians, administrators, and even patients—would also wear the badges.

In that setting, the hospital records system would recognize that a doctor had entered the patient's room and relevant charts would automatically pop up on the computer screen. If someone approached the screen who wasn't authorized to see the patient information, it would go blank. The BadgePAD would know when the doctor put it down; if someone else picked it up, it would have a whole different set of e-services personalized for that person.

This technology is part of HP's vision for the future where people, places, and things are always connected to the Web. It's called CoolTown. Box 11.2 illustrates how this might work. "When you think about connectivity, anything becomes possible—the only limitation is your imagination," says Dick Lampman, director of HP Labs.

One of the greatest innovations to come out of HP Labs is the e-speak services broker. If you think the kinds of changes the CoolTown technology can bring about are big, then consider this one final prediction:

Box 11.2. Life in CoolTown

It's morning in CoolTown, and you've set your alarm clock for 6 A.M. to make an 8 A.M. meeting with a client. But this isn't any ordinary town, and this isn't any ordinary clock–it's a smart alarm that's connected to the Internet, and it communicates with an e-service traffic report. The e-service tells your clock there's an accident on the freeway, so the alarm wakes you early. You arrive at your meeting right on time.

You walk into your meeting carrying nothing but your handheld computer. Your presentation is stored on the Web. When a client wants a copy of a diagram, you don't have to go back to your office to fax or e-mail it. The printer in the conference room is a Web appliance. It accesses the Web to get the diagram and it prints the information right there.

While you're wowing your client, your daughter heads off to catch a bus for a class across town. It's raining, but in CoolTown she doesn't have to stand in the rain. She uses a Web access device to find out how far the bus is from her stop. This bus is a Web appliance, with an embedded computer and Web server, a Global Positioning System, and a wireless network for communicating with the Web. It's twenty minutes away from her stop, so your daughter uses her palmtop to access the Web site of the coffee shop across the street and order a double espresso. When she arrives, her coffee's ready and paid for–she authorized the coffee shop to deduct the cost from her checking account.

e-speak has the capability to break all the rules and reinvent the Internet business model all over again. With e-speak, people can use the Web to complete tasks, solve problems, and conduct transactions automatically, with little human intervention.

Trading community models, especially vertical B-to-B hubs, have all been based on the premise that gravity is the winner. Under this model, business on the Net closely resembles the universe in that entities form and the ones that generate the most gravity attract stars, moons, and planets into their orbit. And—looking at the valuations of some B-to-B trading companies—it's clear that Wall Street has rewarded this business model handsomely.

But there's one problem with it going forward to .profit: it is based on the assumption that stars can talk to planets and planets can talk to moons but that unless you build the links one at a time, stars (portals) cannot dynamically contact the planets (suppliers and customers) of the other stars out there. You want to buy a Princess Diana Beanie Baby on eBay? You can, but only if somebody has registered one for sale on eBay.

What e-speak does is shatter that assumption. It allows buyers and sellers to find a service even when the service isn't available on the trading community site. If we'd said in the early 1990s that by the end of the decade anybody would be able to find any data without knowing where it is using a simple intuitive interface called a Web browser, nobody would have believed it. But now everybody knows that HTML and other associated technologies allow users to locate data without the data residing on the site. Now, users can find data anywhere in the world through a browser. Well, it's time for the next, and the much bigger, step. E-speak performs exactly the same function for services. What this means is that you don't have to register that Beanie Baby on eBay or your 10,000 tons of mild sheet steel on e-Steel. They can be found just like your metatagged data can be.

The tagging of services by e-speak will mean they can be discovered and brokered by anyone searching for them. So your service is now available to anybody who is looking for what you've got. Think the Internet changed everything? Think again. This gives the ultimate power to the buyer and the seller, not the intermediary. It creates as near as possible a pure market.

Gravity goes out of the universal window and pure value comes rushing in. The last remaining inefficiencies in the supply chain, the margins retained by the big procurement portals, get disintermediated—and off we all go again inventing new business models to compete and make money. The smart companies will integrate into their trading community site the e-speak services broker so that you can buy or sell anything to anybody, anywhere in the world—and you don't have to connect everything technically and financially to all the other portals in the world. E-speak will do it for you automatically. Now you have a neural network that can broker from node to node to perform a services match. Is this available now? Yes. Is it expensive? As of December 1999 you could download the e-speak code free of charge at www.e-speak.net; tens of thousands of companies already have.

As this new world plays out, and it won't be long, it's a whole new chapter, indeed a whole new book on the Internet economy. All the old rules will be changed and it will prove once again that just when you thought it was safe to go back into the water, you're faced with the most critical moment in your company's life. Is that a competitor-driven tsunami headed toward you or the early indications of the next big wave that you can ride to stay on top? We believe the answer lies in inventing the path to .profit. Want to come along?

ENDNOTES

Chapter 1

1. U.S. Commerce Department Census Bureau, report by Secretary William Daley, March 3, 2000, PR Newswire. The report is based on a poll of 12,000 companies.
2. The Gartner Group, cited in "The Higher Stakes of Business-to-Business," *New York Times,* March 5, 2000, p. 3.
3. In 1999, there were surprises everywhere. As the online E-Commerce Times commented in January 2000, "The *Wall Street Journal* called the Internet an economic 'pipsqueak.' Amazon.com was a book site. America Online had not yet become a retailer." Rob Spiegel, "E-Commerce Explosion Rivals Rise of the Beatles," E-Commerce Times, January 4, 2000, e-commerce.com/.
4. "A New Economy Nightmare: Value America Rode the Internet Up Like a Rocket, and Came Down Like One," *Washington Post,* March 5, 2000, p. H1.
5. David Pottruck and Terry Pearce, *Clicks and Mortar: Passion-Driven Growth in an Internet-Driven World,* San Francisco: Jossey-Bass, 2000.
6. Rob Spiegel, E-Commerce Times, January 26, 2000, e-commerce.com Web site.
7. Chet Dembeck, E-Commerce Times, November 29, 1999, e-commerce.com Web site.
8. Anthony B. Perkins and Michael C. Perkins, *The Internet Bubble: Inside the Overvalued World of High-Tech Stocks—and What You Need to Know About the Coming Shakeout.* New York: HarperBusiness, 1999, p. 85.

Chapter 2

1. "Amid Market's Mania, Warnings About Asia's Internet Future," *International Herald Tribune,* March 2, 2000, p. 11.
2. "Best Car-Buying Sites," *PC Magazine,* March 10, 2000.
3. See http://www.ford.com/default.asp?pageid=106&storyid=674
4. Anitesh Barua and Andrew B. Whinston, "The Emerging Internet Economy" (online slide presentation), 1999. See http://crec.bus.utexas.edu
5. "GM Ready to Provide Internet Access in Some Cars," *San Jose Mercury News,* quoted in SiliconValley.com, November 2, 1999.
6. According to the University of Texas, Austin. See http://crec.bus.utexas.edu
7. Peter G. W. Keen, *Competing in Chapter 2 of Internet Business: Navigating in a New World,* The Netherlands: TUDelft, 1999.
8. Geoffrey A. Moore, Paul Johnson, and Tom Kippola, *The Gorilla Game,* New York: HarperBusiness, 1998.
9. Phil Harvey, "Cisco's Secret for Success," March 6, 2000. See www.redherring.com

Chapter 3

1. Our economic figures have been gathered from far too many sources to list: hundreds of reported surveys from industry associations, research reports, company statements, Web site searches, the business and Internet trade press, and academic studies over a three-year period. Some of the specific figures are referenced in several of Peter Keen's books, including *Online Profits, The Business Internet and Intranets, The Process Edge,* and *Building Electronic Commerce Relationships.*
2. Cern Basher, "Accounting for a New Economy," Provident Investment Advisers E-Mail Reports, March 6, 2000, provident.listbot.com.
3. Stuart Elliott, "The Media Business: Advertising; The Super Bowl Is Attracting a Crowd of New Competitors," *New York Times,* November 28, 1999.
4. Robert H. Miles and Gil Amelio, *Corporate Comeback: The Story of Renewal and Transformation at National Semiconductor,* San Francisco: Jossey-Bass, 1997.
5. Marci McDonald, "You Haven't Got Mail: Big Firms Fail to Answer Consumer E-Queries," USNews Online, February 28, 2000.
6. This information was drawn from personal communications as a consultant.
7. This information was drawn from personal communications as a consultant.
8. For a fuller discussion of the costs of pre-Internet information technology infrastructures, see Peter Keen, *Shaping the Future,* Cambridge, Mass.: Harvard Business School Press, Chapter 6, "Managing the Costs of IT Capital."

While the figures have changed, the dynamics remain constant for the era of large-scale "mission-critical" Internet business operations.

Chapter 4
1. We refer to Chemdex here instead of using its more recent name, Ventro, because that was its name when it launched these initiatives. Chemdex is the name used in our sources.
2. Joelle Tessler, "Chemdex Teams Up with Tenet E-Commerce, Not ER: New Form Will Hook Up Hospitals to Medical Suppliers," *San Jose Mercury News,* December 14, 1999, p. 3C.

Chapter 5
1. From company Web site www.ariba.com
2. Sandor Boyson, Thomas M. Corsi, Martin E. Dresner, and Lisa H. Harrington, *Logistics and the Extended Enterprise: Benchmarks and Best Practices for the Manufacturing Professional,* New York: Wiley, 1999, pp. 135–138.
3. Robert Wayman, "The Bottom Line or Supply Chain Management." Presentation to i2 Planet conference, October 10–13, 1999, Las Vegas, Nevada.
4. Bruce Caldwell, "Reverse Logistics—Untapped Opportunities Exist in Returned Products, a Side of Logistics Few Businesses Have Thought About—Until Now," *Information Week,* April 12, 1999.
5. Peter G. W. Keen, *Shaping the Future—Business Design Through Information Technology,* Cambridge, Mass.: Harvard Business School Press, 1991.
6. Peter Fabris, *CIO Magazine,* June 15, 1997.
7. See "I Heard It Through the Grapevine . . ." http://www.americanbusiness press.com/resources/Committees/BrnadExtension/NewPage69111.html
8. Peter Keen, "IT's Value in the Chain," *Computerworld,* February 2000.
9. Peter Keen, *Online Profits: A Manager's Guide to Electronic Commerce,* Cambridge, Mass.: Harvard Business School Press, 1997.
10. Mary Hillebrand, "Commerce Giants Launch International B2B Hub," E-Commerce Times, February 11, 2000, e-commerce.com Web site.
11. See www.fool.com

Chapter 6
1. Robert D. Hof in San Mateo, Calif., with Gary McWilliams in Houston and Gabrielle Saveri in San Francisco, "Overview: The 'Click Here' Economy," *Business Week,* June 22, 1998; and Joann Muller in Detroit, with Keith Naughton in Detroit and Larry Armstrong in Los Angeles, *Business Week,* "Old Carmakers Learn New Tricks," April 12, 1999.

2. *Future Banker,* May 1999, p. 28.

3. Wells Fargo's cost for providing teller service is $1.07, versus the ATM cost of $0.27 (and Internet cost of $0.01). That's great. But if, instead of cashing one check a week for $250, a customer makes five withdrawals of $50 each, it's a wash. This is why one of the regular features of ATM service in the 1980s—being able to use the machine just to check your account balance—is a rarity now. When this was part of the menu of options, most people automatically chose it. See George Foster, Mahendra Gupta, and Richard Palmer, "Cases in Strategic-Systems Auditing Business-to-Business Electronic Commerce," KPMG/University of Illinois Business Measurement Case Development and Research Program Web site: http://www.cba.uiuc.edu/kpmg-uiuc/cases/fargo/fargo.htm

4. Andy Wang, "Amazon Reports Rise in Revenues and Losses," E-Commerce Times, October 28, 1999, e-commerce.com Web site.

5. Megan Barnett, "Online Brokers Eat Their Own Dog Food: Investors Have Turned Their Attention to Net Brokerage Stocks, Bidding Them Up Dramatically. Coming next: Acquisitions and Spin-Offs," *Standard,* February 5, 1999.

6. louise@ft.com, "INSIDE TRACK: Traditional Values Win in Online Store Wars," *Financial Times,* July 14, 1999. Note, however, that this .com did not make money and in mid-2000 looked likely to fold.

7. Peter G. W. Keen, "Relationships: The Electronic Commerce Imperative," www.peterkeen.com, March 1, 2000.

8. Keen, "Relationships."

9. Keen, "Relationships."

10. "Altered Relationships," *Information Week,* June 21, 1999, p. 20ss. Source is given as Lisa Richard, VP of strategic business planning, Toshiba America.

11. Press Release, February 16, 1999, www.dell.com

12. Cern Basher, "Ariba—Changing the Way the World Does Business," January 19, 2000, e-mail to Provident Bank customers.

13. Scott Rosenberg, "Yahoo Buys GeoCities—Pop-up Ads and All," January 29, 1999, www.salon.com

14. Ajit Kambli, G. Bruce Friesen, and Arul Sundaram, "Co-Creation: A New Source of Value," *Outlook,* 1999, No. 2, p. 38.

15. The papers "Plattformen und Gemeinschaften von Agenten—Eine Architektur von Medien," by Martina Klose, Ulrike Lechner, Beat Schmid, and Katarina Stanoevska, and "Anwendung des Medienmodells und Medienreferenzmodells—Case Study Amazon.com," by Martina Klose, Ulrike Lechner, Olga Miler, Petra Schubert, and Beat Schmid, have been accepted at Gemeinschaften in neuen Medien (GeNeMe99) http://www-emw.inf.tu-dresden.de/geneme/

16. Robert D. Hof and Peter Elstrom, "Internet Communities," *Business Week,* May 12, 1999.
17. Hof and Elstrom, "Internet Communities."
18. Hof and Elstrom, "Internet Communities."
19. Hof and Elstrom, "Internet Communities."
20. For example, Owners.Com is a hub for FSBOs (properties for sale by owner); Realtor.Com, the National Association of Realtors' hub, provides 1.2 million listings from agents; Homebid.Com offers online auctions for repossessed and foreclosed properties.

Chapter 7

1. "The Internet Is Crushing Whole Industries. . . . Is Your Company Next?" *PC Computing,* February 2000.
2. *Financial Times,* December 16, 1999, p. 18.
3. "Retailers' Resentment Grows with Online Sales," *USA Today,* November 10, 1999, p. 3B.
4. *Red Herring,* July 1999, p. 78.
5. *Gartner Executive Edge,* September 1999.
6. *Computerworld,* December 13, 1999, p. 54.
7. Gibson's Web site manager, quoted in *CIO Web Business,* February 1998.

Chapter 8

1. Provident Bank, e-mail announcement to customers, September 29, 1999.
2. Geoffrey A. Moore, Paul Johnson, and Tom Kippola, *The Gorilla Game,* New York: HarperBusiness, 1998.
3. See www.bizrate.com
4. Source for all three bullet points is Anthony B. Perkins and Michael C. Perkins, *The Internet Bubble: Inside the Overvalued World of High-Tech Stocks—and What You Need to Know to Avoid the Coming Shakeout,* New York: HarperBusiness, 1999.

Chapter 9

1. Peter G. W. Keen, *Competing in Chapter 2 of Internet Business: Navigating in a New World,* The Netherlands: TUDelft, 1999.
2. Joseph Kahn, "The On-Line Brokerage Battle," *New York Times,* October 4, 1999, p. C19.
3. Keen, *Competing in Chapter 2 of Internet Business.*
4. Mark Halper, "Making Money on the Web," *CIO Magazine,* January 15, 1998.
5. Kahn, "The On-Line Brokerage Battle."

6. EVA underlies much of Peter Keen's work on the economics of information technology, business processes, and Internet business. His major and strongly recommended source of ideas here is Bennett Stewart's indispensable book *The Quest for Value: The EVA Management Guide,* New York: HarperBusiness, 1991.

7. Tony Perkins, "The Angler," *Red Herring,* April 1999, p. 14.

Chapter 10

1. *Business 2.0,* March 1999.
2. *Interactive Week,* April 23, 1998.
3. *Gartner Executive Edge,* June/July 1999.
4. *Business 2.2,* April 1999.
5. *Business 2.0,* December 1999, p. 285.
6. *Business 2.0,* December 1999, p. 285.
7. *Business 2.0,* December 1999, p. 285.

Chapter 11

1. Mary Meeker, Morgan Stanley press release 1.0, March 13, 2000.
2. Peter D. Henig, "And Now, Econets," *Red Herring,* February 2000.
3. Release 1.0, March 13, 2000.
4. Stewart Alsop, "Bye Bye Music Business," *Fortune,* 2000, *141*(6), 72.
5. Jon Healey and Sara Robinson, "Major Label Plans to Sell Music Online," *San Jose Mercury News,* April 6, 2000. http://www.sjmercury.com/business/top/009727.htm.
6. See the International Data Corporation Web site: www.idc.com.

INDEX